Helion & Company Limited
Unit 8 Amherst Business Centre
Budbrooke Road
Warwick
CV34 5WE
England
Tel. 01926 499 619
Email: info@helion.co.uk
Website: www.helion.co.uk
Twitter: @helionbooks
Visit our blog http://blog.helion.co.uk/

Photographs: Unless stated otherwise, all the photographs used in this volume have been obtained in the form of prints from the Military Museum of Hanoi and the Vietnam News Agency in the Socialist Republic of Vietnam. In turn, these have been sourced from official agencies in the USSR/Russia, including the Ministry of Defence in Moscow, and various news agencies.

Designed and typeset by Farr out Publications, Wokingham, Berkshire
Cover design by Paul Hewitt, Battlefield Design (www.battlefield-design.co.uk)

ISBN 978-1-914059-06-3

British Library Cataloguing-in-Publication Data
A catalogue record for this book is available from the British Library

We always welcome receiving book proposals from prospective authors.

Contents

Note: In order to simplify the use of this book, all names, locations and geographic designations are as provided in *The Times World Atlas*, or other traditionally accepted major sources of reference, as of the time of described events. Correspondingly, the term 'Congo' designates the area of the former Belgian colony of the Congo Free State, granted independence as the Democratic Republic of the Congo in June 1960 and in use until 1971 when the country was renamed Republic of Zaire, which, in turn, reverted to Democratic Republic of the Congo in 1997, and which remains in use today. As such, Congo is not to be mistaken for the former French colony of Middle Congo (Moyen Congo), officially named the Republic of the Congo on its independence in August 1960, also known as Congo-Brazzaville.

Abbreviations

ABAKO	Alliance of Bakongo (Congo)
ANC	African National Congress (South Africa)
ANC	Armée Nationale Congolaise
APC	Armoured Personnel Carrier
BOSS	Bureau of State Security (South Africa)
CGT	General Confederation of Labour (France)
CIR	Centros de Instrucción Revolucionaria
COAN	Argentine Naval Aviation
DRC	Democratic Republic of the Congo
DEA	Drug Enforcement Agency (USA)
ELNA	National Liberation Army of Angola
ELP	Portuguese Liberation Army (Angola)
FAP	Portuguese Air Force
FAPLA	Popular Armed Forces for the Liberation of Angola
FAR	Cuban Revolutionary Armed Forces
FBI	Federal Bureau of Investigation
FDLA	Democratic Front for the Liberation of Angola
FLS	Frontline States
FNL	National Liberation Front (Algeria)
FNLA	National Liberation Front of Angola
FRELIMO	Mozambique Liberation Front (Frente de Libertação de Moçambique)
GRAE	Revolutionary Government of Angola in Exile
HVAR	High Velocity Aircraft Rockets
IFP	Inkatha Freedom Party (South Africa)
IGA	Inter-departmental Group for Africa
ISO	International Security Organisation (PMC set up by John Banks in 1975)
MINA	Movement for the National Independence of Angola
MFA	Armed Forces Movement (Portugal)
MMCA	Cuban Military Mission in Angola
MPLA	People's Movement for the Liberation of Angola
MLSTP	Movement for the Liberation of São Tomé and Principe
NATO	North Atlantic Treaty Organisation
NME	National Military Establishment
NSA	National Security Agency (USA)
NSC	National Security Council (USA)
NSJ	National Salvation Junta (Portugal)
NSSM	National Security Study Memorandum
OAPEC	Organisation of Arab Petroleum Exporting Countries
OAU	Organisation of African Unity
PAIGC	African Party for the Independence of Guinea and Cape Verde
PCA	Angolan Communist Party
PCI	Italian Communist Party
PCP	Portuguese Communist Party
PDRA	Popular Democratic Republic of Angola
PLAN	People's Liberation Army of Namibia
PMC	Private Military Company
PRA	People's Republic of Angola
PRC	People's Republic of China
PLUA	Party of the United Struggle for Africans in Angola
RAMC	Royal Army Medical Corps
RhAF	Rhodesian Air Force
SAAF	South African Air Force
SADF	South African Defence Force
SALT	Strategic Arms Limitation Talks
SAM	Surface-to-Air Missile
SAS	Special Advisory Services (the second PMC created by John Banks in 1975)
SAS	Special Air Service (UK)
SBS	Special Boat Service (UK)
SDECE	Service de Documentation Extérieure et du Contre-Espionnage (France)
SID	Servizio Informazione Difesa (Italy)
SIS	Secret Intelligence Service (MI6)
SOG	Special Operations Group
SWANU	South West Africa National Union
SWALA	South West Africa Liberation Army
SWAPO	South West Africa People's Organisation
UDR	Ulster Defence Regiment
UNITA	National Union for the Total Independence of Angola
UNPA	Union of Peoples of Northern Angola
UPA	United Peoples of Angola
USIC	United States Intelligence Community
UVF	Ulster Volunteer Force

Introduction

Following previous studies produced for Helion on the roots and dynamics of the Congo Crisis, the intention of this current volume is to throw light on CIA clandestine operations that took place in Angola in 1975/1976. The operations known collectively as IA/FEATURE, they involved an attempt by the CIA and friendly forces such as South Africa to influence the outcome of the Angolan Civil War (1974-1976) and to put in place a regime considered as friendly to US strategic and economic interests. This support for two Angolan movements, the FNLA and UNITA, fitting into wider considerations linked to the notions of containment and *real politik*, the United States government under Gerald Ford funded a programme whereby thousands of tons of weapons were shipped through Zaire in order to combat nationalist armed forces backed by Cuba and the Soviet Union. In contrast to the success of clandestine operations in the Congo, Operation IA/FEATURE proved to be an unmitigated failure. Effectively, we will see that in spite of massive quantities of arms there was a shortage of manpower trained to use them. To resolve this problem, US national security advisors turned to the use of mercenaries and began the direct recruitment of Portuguese and French mercenaries. Without the CIA's knowledge, FNLA leader Holden Roberto was using millions of dollars of CIA money to fund his own private army of British mercenaries. Led by the now infamous "Colonel Callan", a small number of these mercenaries used the Angolan context as an excuse to exact brutal punishments and murder on not only the local population, but also on other British mercenaries. As we shall see, these activities contributed to bringing IA/FEATURE to a halt and put an end to US ambitions of seeing communism defeated in Angola. A tale that contains a series of twists and turns, this volume provides an insight into the inner-workings of US clandestine operations and the events that influenced high-level US decision-making in the mid-1970s.

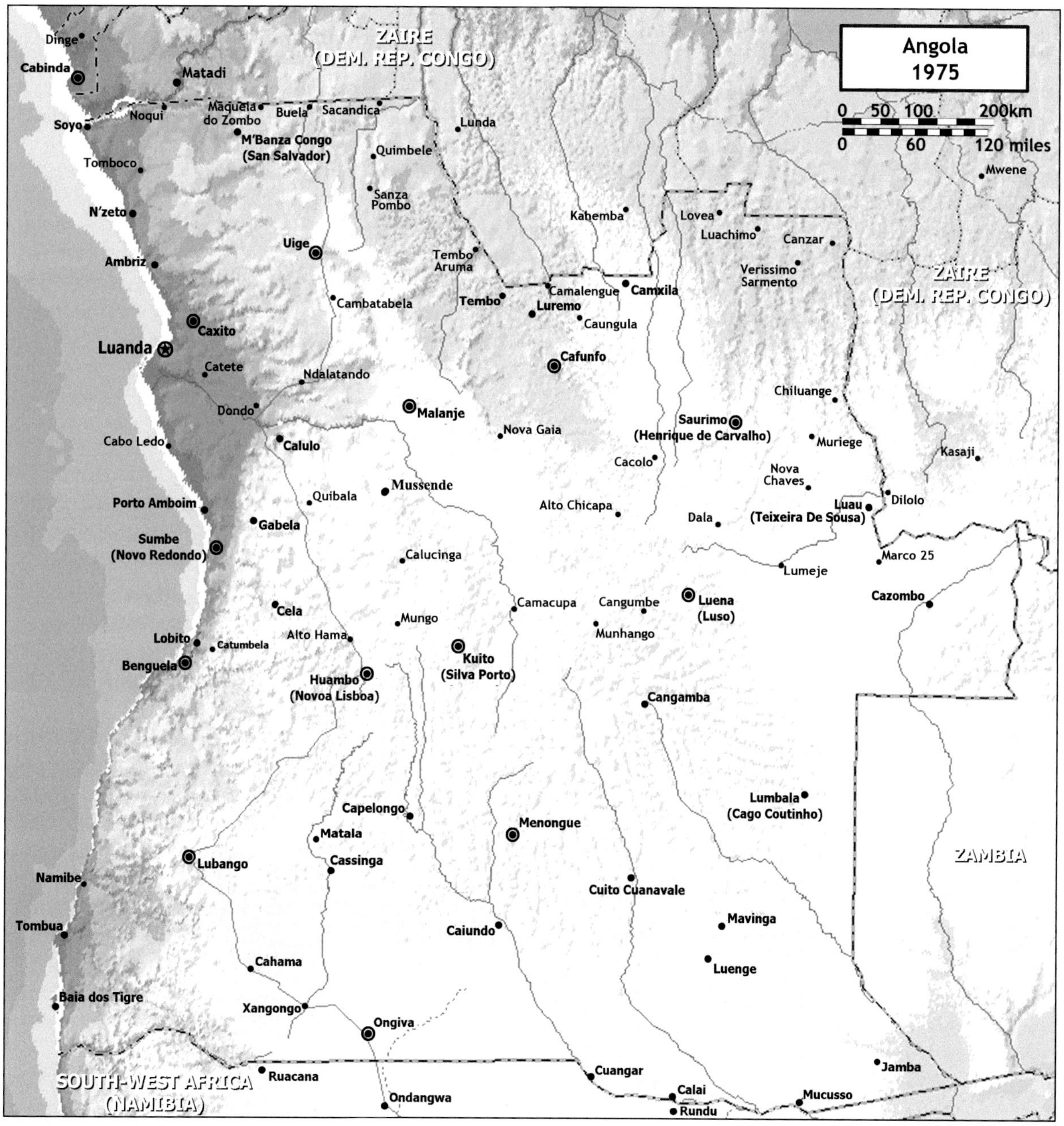

Angola of 1975. (Map by Tom Cooper)

Timeline of Angola, 1480s – 1970s

1480s – Portuguese explorer Diego Cão makes two voyages along the west coast of Africa reaching the area currently known as Angola around 1483. Cão was the first European to sight and enter the River Congo and during this time he began trade with natives from the Bakongo tribe. Portuguese slave trading started around this time.

1636 – The arrival of King Alvaro VI and his brother Garcia II signals the beginning of war between the Bakongo Kingdom and Portuguese settlers.

1665 – Portuguese forces defeat the forces of the Bakongo Kingdom and some of its captured nobles are transported to Brazil. Most slaves are transported to Brazil from ports in Luanda and Benguela.

1808 – The Blockade of Africa gradually sees an end to the Atlantic slave trade. Between 1808 and 1860, the British West Africa Squadron seized approximately 1,600 slave ships and freed around 150,000 Africans bound for the Americas.

1833 – Slavery is abolished in the UK through the Slavery Abolition Act. Portugal bans slavery in 1836.

1884/1885 – The Berlin Conference sees Portugal acquire the left bank of the Congo River. Several agreements are concluded between Belgium and France from 1886-1984 and by the end of the 19th century most of Angola was recognised as a Portuguese possession. In 1885, the Portuguese also signed the Treaty of Simulambuco with officials from the N'Goyo Kingdom giving the Angolan exclave of Cabinda the status of protectorate of the Portuguese Crown.

1926 – Portugal reaffirms its authority over Angola after a military putsch on 28 May puts an end to the Portuguese First Republic and sees the beginning of the *Estado Novo* (New State).

1932 – Antonio Salazar becomes Prime Minister of Portugal.

1941 – The Atlantic Charter states that all people had the right to self-determination.

1945 – The United Nations is created and states that its intention is to strive for the promotion of peace by promoting self-determination.

1951 – Portugal's constitution is revised and all its overseas possessions are incorporated into the Portuguese state.

1953 – The foundation of the Party of the United Struggle for Africans in Angola (PLUA).

1954 – The foundation of the Union of Peoples of Northern Angola (UPNA).

1955 – The foundation of the Angolan Communist Party (PCA).

1956 – The foundation of the Movement for the Liberation of Angola (MPLA) in December.

1957 – The Gold Coast becomes the first sub-Saharan nation to gain its independence from a colonial power. It becomes Ghana and its first president is Kwame Nkrumah.

1959 – The foundation of the United Peoples of Angola (UPA).

1961 – Riots against Portuguese authority start in early January. They are repressed by Portuguese forces.

1961 – In March, Portuguese settlers are massacred by UPA forces calling themselves the National Liberation Army of Angola (ELNA). Some receive training from the Algerian National Liberation Front (FNL).

The Democratic Party of Angola (PDA) merges with the UPA to form the National Front for the Liberation of Angola (FNLA).

1962 – Based in Congo-Léopoldville, the FNLA declares that it is the only legitimate government in Angola and forms the Revolutionary Government of Angola in Exile (GRAE). The movement is led by Holden Roberto and its Foreign Minister is Jonas Savimbi.

1964 – Jonas Savimbi resigns from the GRAE and travels to the People's Republic of China for training in military theories.

1965 – Neto meets Ernesto Guevara in Brazzaville.

1966 – Savimbi creates the National Union for the Total Independence of Angola (UNITA). He receives military assistance from China from this point.

1968 – Marcello Caetano become Portugal's Prime Minister on 27 September.

1974 – The Carnation Revolution takes place in Portugal on 25 April. General Antonio de Spínola emerges as the head of the National Salvation Junta (JSN).

- The FNLA greets a contingent of Chinese military advisors and receives weapons from Communist-bloc countries.
- The Soviet Union begins to step up arms transfers to the MPLA in September and October of this year and they are used by its military wing, the People's Armed Forces of Angola (FAPLA).
- Portuguese Guinea gains its independence in September 1974 and becomes Guinea-Bissau.

1975 – In January, the Alvor Agreements see a date set for the independence of Angola.

- Soviet arms transfers to the MPLA continue and see the appearance of tanks, fighter aircraft and Katyusha rocket launchers.
- In May, Cuba sends 230 advisors to train the MPLA.
- In early June an MPLA delegation visits Moscow in an unsuccessful attempt to obtain direct Soviet involvement in the Angolan Civil War.
- Also in June, Neto meets with members of the Cuban Mission and the Central Committee.
- In June and July clashes between supporters of the MPLA and UNITA take place in Luanda. In late July, the FAPLA advances into UNITA areas.
- In the summer, President Giscard d'Estaing of France visits Zaire and discusses the question of military assistance to anti-MPLA forces with Roberto.
- In July, South African Prime Minister John Vorster authorises the transfer of funds and weapons to the FNLA and UNITA. This arrives in August 1975.
- Also in July, Cuban Military Mission in Angola (MMCA) meets Agostinho Neto, the leader of the MPLA. An agreement is reached whereby MPLA soldiers would be trained by soldiers of the Cuban Revolutionary Armed Forces (FAR). The first Cuban soldiers arrive in Angola in September.
- On 9 August, a 30-man patrol of the South African Defence Force (SADF) moved 50 km. into Angola to

protect the Ruacana-Calueque hydroelectric complex and other industrial installations along the Cunene River. The defence of these installations is used by South Africa to justify military intervention.

- South Africa launches Operation Sausage II on 22 August. This is a major operation against the South West Africa People's Organisation (SWAPO).
- On 4 September, South African Prime Minister John Vorster offers limited military support to the FNLA and UNITA.
- In early September five Cuban merchant ships leave Havana bound for Angola. They carry troops, ammunition and weapons.
- By early October, the South African Defence Force (SADF) appoints a number of its officers to provide training to UNITA forces. They set up training camps around Silva Porto and assemble the mobile attack group named Task Force Foxbat. The group's first encounter with FAPLA forces takes place on 5 October. Around the same time, the five Cuban ships arrive after a three-week voyage. Cubana Airlines begins airlifts to Angola.
- Operation Savannah is launched from South West Africa on 14 October, the objective being to expel MPLA forces from southern and eastern Angola. The objective is to eliminate MPLA presence from southern areas of Angola.
- In mid-October, the French SDECE sends money to the FNLA. French secret services work alongside the CIA and Mobutu.
- On 5 November, Cuba begins Operation Carlota in support of the MPLA. The objective is to defeat South African forces as well as the FNLA which is supported by Zairian troops sent by Mobutu.
- The Battle of Quifangondo on 10 November is the FNLA's last opportunity to defeat the MPLA and stop Neto from becoming president.
- The FNLA's loss sees the MPLA become the legitimate power as Angola becomes an independent nation on 11 November.

1
Angola, a Short Presentation

Portuguese explorer Diego Cão was the first European known to have sighted and entered the Congo River sometime around 1483, the area known as current-day Angola had long been settled by the San people, a hunter-gatherer group whose territories extended across large tracts of southern Africa. Later, having been joined by Bantu-speaking peoples from more central and northern regions, the Kingdom of the Kongo was set up in the 14th century and rapidly became Africa's first large political entity stretching from Gabon to the north, to the River Kwanza in the south, and to the River Cuango in the east. The name of the kingdom deriving from the Kikongo language spoken by most of its inhabitants, its early economy was fuelled mainly by agriculture but as the years went by it gradually grew into one of the main centres for the Atlantic slave trade.

Although the kingdom managed to stave off Portuguese incursions up to the mid-1630s, the arrival of King Alvaro VI in 1636, then his brother Garcia II of Kongo signalled the beginning of a period during which wars between the kingdom and Portuguese settlers in the region created long-lasting rivalries.[1] These wars such as the Battle of Mbwila in 1665 were to lead to a state of near anarchy in the kingdom and internal struggles between the different kings of the Kongo's provinces eventually led to the complete collapse of the kingdom. Ultimately, it was not political dispute that led to the end of the Kingdom of the Kongo but economic pressure brought on by the British abolishing the slave trade thus cutting off the kingdom's principal source of income.[2] With the economy in ruins and the kingdom's large cities having been mostly abandoned by traders, what was left of a once powerful African political entity was divided up and handed over to Portugal and Belgium at the Berlin Conference of 1884-1885. In February 1885, the Portuguese government also signed the Treaty of Simulambuco with officials from the N'Goyo Kingdom giving the Angolan exclave of Cabinda the status of protectorate of the Portuguese Crown.

In spite of anti-Portuguese sentiment expressed by the Ovimbundu, on 28 May 1926, Portugal was to affirm its colonial authority after a military putsch put an end to the Portuguese First Republic and initiated a 48-year period of National Dictatorship. Soon to evolve into the *Estado Novo* led by Antonio de Oliveira Salazar, from 1932 Portugal consolidated a programme whereby the doctrine of lusotropicalism dictated Portuguese oversees policy. Seeing itself as a pluricontinental entity and guided by three essential moral notions (God, Fatherland, and Family), the 1933 constitution was revised in 1951 and stated that all of Portugal's possessions were officially incorporated into the Portuguese state. The revision reiterated the sentiment that it was Portugal's duty was "to fulfill its historic mission of colonisation" and "to diffuse among the populations inhabiting its territories the benefits of Portuguese civilisation".[3]

Though its ambitions were similar to those of other European colonisers in that the African population was to be assimilated into the European population, Portugal's being one of the poorest nations in Europe at the time meant that it lacked the financial means to implement the type of social reforms carried out in the neighbouring Belgian Congo. According to the 1950 census, 135,355 of Angola's population of 4,009,911 had become *assimilados* or "civilised", and of that number 78,826 were white, 26,355 of mixed race and only 30,039 Africans. *Assimilados* had rights such as travelling freely inside Angola, being able to obtain a passport, the right to vote and the right to free education. He was also exempt from forced labour but had to pay taxes and lost the right to free medical services and the right to have several wives.[4] For the remainder of the Angolan population, it was classed as *indigena* or "a person of the Negro race who is governed by the

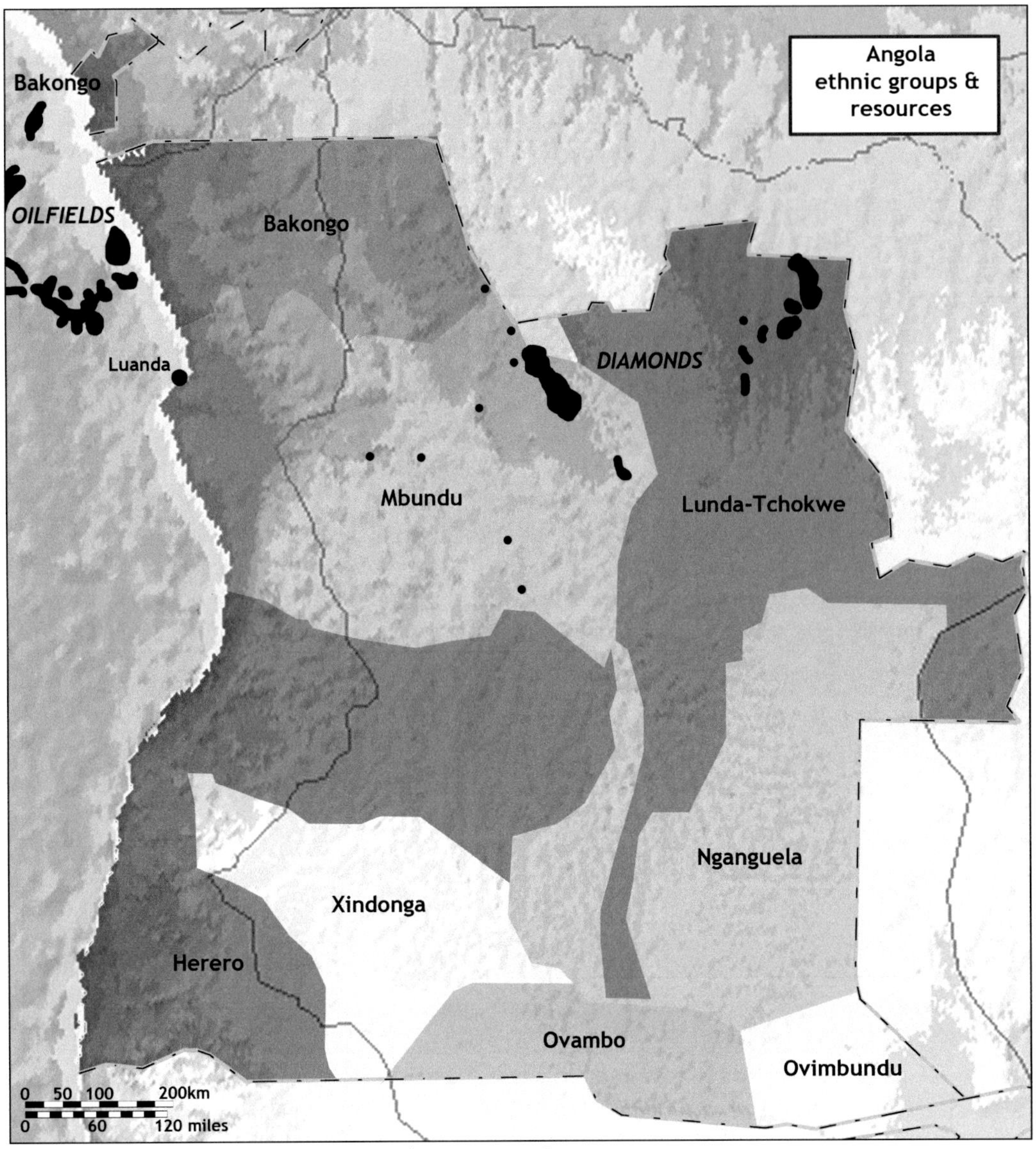

Angola's ethnic groups and resources. (Map by Tom Cooper)

customs of his own society and has not yet evolved to a cultural level which would permit him to be governed by the same laws as a Portuguese citizen".[5] An *indigena* had no political rights, nor could he hope that his situation may change rapidly. For the one percent of the Angolan population that attended school,[6] however, there were opportunities to go on to secondary schooling and eventually to university. This was the case for almost all of the Angolan political figures who emerged in the 1950s.

While we will see more of Angola's political struggles of the 1950s, 1960s and 1970s in other parts of this volume, what we can say about the country today is that the territory now known as the Republic of Angola covers a surface of some one and a quarter million square miles of southern Africa. It is situated on the continent's Atlantic coast and bordering Namibia, the Democratic Republic of the Congo and Zambia, and the country also comprises Cabinda, an exclave bordering the Republic of the Congo. At slightly less than twice the size of Texas and slightly less than one-tenth of the size of Europe, Angola's narrow coastal plain stretches along 1,600 kilometres while the remainder of the country is perched upon plateaux and highlands such as the Bié Plateau to the east of the capital city Luanda, the Huila Plateau in the south, and the Malanje Highlands situated in the north-central part of the country. The highest point in Angola can be found at Mount Moco near the city of Huambo, and this peak reaches some 2,260 metres. Around 65 percent of Angola is situated 1,000 to 1,600 metres above sea level but a rich network of around 30 rivers including the Congo, the Cuanza and the Cubango provide fresh water for the growing of marketed cash crops such as coffee, cotton and sisal or food crops such as bananas, citrus fruits, millet and rice. Employing over 70 percent of Angola's population, the agricultural sector is joined by other primary sector industries including the mining of copper, gold, platinum and uranium. Angola's hydroelectric potential is one of the largest in Africa but it is alluvial diamonds, oil and, more recently, gas, that produce a large portion of Angola's revenue. The production of oil comes almost entirely from offshore fields off the coast of Cabinda while other oil-rich areas are situated in the deepwater fields of the Lower Congo Basin.

As is the case with almost all African countries, Angola's ethnic landscape is varied and its population speaks a variety of languages. Nearly 500 years of Portuguese presence in Angola means that it is known by approximately 80 percent of the population, but it is the six Bantu languages (Umbundu, Kimbundu, Kikongo, Chockwe, Kwanyama, and Ngangela) which are the most widely spoken. Otherwise, another 42 languages make up Angola's linguistic landscape.[7] In terms of who speaks these languages, Angola's population is around 32.5 million, and in terms of who speaks which language the Umbundu-speaking Ovimbundu make up the largest ethnic group in Angola at some 37 percent of the population. Other large ethnic groups are the Kimbundu (25 percent), and the Bakaongo (13 percent).[8] Ranked 149th out of 189 countries on the Human Development Index (HDI), over 50 percent of Angola's population live in multidimensional poverty while life expectancy is estimated at just under 60 years for males and slightly over 60 years for females. This places Angola 213th out of 228 countries listed by the CIA's World Factbook.[9]

2
From Independence to Civil War

The Road to Angolan Independence

The Inter-Allied Meeting and the subsequent Declaration of St. Jame's Palace issued on 12 June 1941 marked the first step on the road to self-determination for nations still under colonial administration. Signed by the governments of the United Kingdom, Canada, Australia, New Zealand and South Africa as well as representatives of the provisional governments of Czechoslovakia, Yugoslavia, Greece, Norway, The Netherlands and by the leader of Free French forces, Charles de Gaulle, the agreement resolved that the struggle against the Axis powers would continue until victory was won and that there could be no settled peace as long as peoples were coerced into submission. Peace could only come when peoples free from the threat of aggression were able to work together with the objective of ensuring economic and social security.[1] Being signed at a time when US supply ships were coming under regular attack along North Atlantic shipping routes, the next phase in the development of postwar geopolitical stratagems came with the signing of an agreement by Roosevelt and Churchill at Placentia Bay on 14 August 1941. Effectively, though Lend-Lease was bound to be a prominent feature of the talks given the Axis was still very much in the ascendant and that Great Britain needed to replenish its wartime stocks, how the world would be remodelled once hostilities had ceased were outlined using eight points contained in the so-called "Atlantic Charter". As well as including statements on the "Basic Principles of International Justice" or on the requirement for the "fullest collaboration between all nations in the economic field", both the United States and Great Britain pledged that they would not seek to extend their respective territories that did not accord with the wishes of the peoples concerned. Furthermore, they both agreed that sovereign rights should be restored "to those who have been forcibly deprived of them".[2] What followed Churchill's return to London was a pledge of cooperation signed on 24 September 1941 by 10 other nations including the Soviet Union and subsequent agreements to provide mutual support given at the Tehran Conference of November 1943, the Dumbarton Oaks Conference held in Washington D.C. in 1944, and the Yalta Conference of February 1945. As the Second World War was drawing to a close, the spirit of international unity that had been created over the past four years resulted in the representatives of 46 nations attending the United Nations Conference on International Organisation held in San Francisco from 25 April to 26 June 1945. Otherwise known as the San Francisco Conference, participants made a commitment to maintain peace and security, to achieve international cooperation, to provide a forum at which international disputes might be settled. What was most relevant for nations still under colonial domination was Chapter XI, Article 73 of an agreement known as the United Nations Charter. This article stated that its member nations would strive to develop self-determination and take into account the political aspirations of peoples and assist them in the development of free political institutions.[3]

From the end of the Second World War, a number of countries soon benefited from British and French desires (and needs) to grant independence to colonial possessions. Vietnam, India, Pakistan, Burma (now Myanmar), Ceylon (now Sri Lanka), Malaya (now Malaysia) were among the Asian beneficiaries while France's northern African colonies of Tunisia and Morocco were also relatively early in joining the roll call of independent nations. Though Sudan in North-East Africa became independent in December 1956, only after Britain and France had thrown in the towel at Suez a month or so earlier did they realise that their respective colonial ambitions in sub-Saharan Africa would have to be abandoned. Their doing so led to the independence of the Gold Coast (Ghana) in March 1957 and a subsequent period of 11 years during which no fewer than 33 nations formerly under British, French, Belgian or Spanish control became self-governing. Among the European nations that had previously maintained some form of metropolitan influence in African colonies, the black sheep, so to speak, was Portugal. Despite becoming a member of the United Nations in December 1955, Portugal refused to give up its territories of Angola, Mozambique, Portuguese Guinea (Guinea-Bissau) and Cape Verde, and had even amended its constitution in 1952 as a means of mounting a legal challenge against the UN's definition of what represented a colony. Indeed, Portugal contended that the aforementioned possessions were not colonies but overseas provinces that were politically inseparable from the mainland.[4]

Daniel Chipenda was the leader of a faction of the MPLA called the Eastern Revolt. He later became a political opponent of MPLA leader Agostinho Neto and in March 1975, Chipenda and his followers defected to the FNLA. (Author's collection)

Angolan Resistance to Portuguese Rule: the three main political movements

In a similar fashion to concurrent developments taking place in neighbouring Belgian Congo war found its roots in the actions of underground political movements created in the 1950s. Among them, the Party of the United Struggle for Africans in Angola (PLUA) founded in 1953, the Angolan Communist Party (PCA)

Holden Roberto

Date of birth: 12 January 1923
Place of birth: São Salvador, now known as Mbanza Congo in northern Angola.
Parents and family: Garcia Diasiwa Roberto and Joana Lala Nekaka. Family moved to Leopoldville in 1925 where his father worked in the Finance Ministry of the Belgian colonial administration. Married to a relative of Mobutu Sese Soko.
Education: In 1940, Roberto graduated from a Baptist mission school then worked at the Finance Ministry in Leopoldville (now Kinshasa), Costermansville (now Bukavu) and Stanleyville (now Kisangani).
Political career: After seeing an old man being abused by Portuguese officials, in 1954 Roberto founded the Union of Peoples of Northern Angola (UPNA), later the Union of Peoples of Angola (UPA), with his uncle, Sydney Manuel Barros Nekaka. As a representative of the UPA, in 1958 Roberto attended the All-African Peoples' Conference in Accra, Ghana. Here, he met Patrice Lumumba, Kenneth Kuanda and Jomo Kenyatta. In March 1962, Roberto's UPA merged with the Democratic Party of Angola to form the Revolutionary Government of Angola in Exile (GRAE). From the 1961, Roberto received payments from the United States Security Council to provide intelligence and is paid a retainer of $10,000 per year. In 1962 President Kennedy is advised to choose Roberto as a link between the United States and indigenous Angolan groups as it is believed that Portugal will soon be forced out of Angola. From 1962 to 1969, the US provides money and arms to Roberto. In 1969, Roberto is "deactivated". In 1973, Roberto visits the PRC and Dong Biwu subsequently sends 119 military advisors to train the FNLA.
Date of death: 2 August 2007

FNLA leader Holden Roberto was related to Mobutu through marriage and set up his political base in the Congolese capital. (Prabook)

Agostinho Neto

Date of birth: 17 September 1922
Place of birth: Icolo e Bengo (situated in Catete area near Luanda)
Heritage: Mbundu
Parents: Agostinho Pedro, a clergyman and Maria, a kindergarten teacher.
Education and personal life: Attended Liceu Salvador Correia High School then Coimbra University (Portugal) from 1947 to study medicine and graduated in 1951. Here, he met Amilcar Cabral from Guinea-Bissau and Marcelino dos Santos from Mozambique. Together they formed the Anti-Colonial Movement with the objective of opposing Portuguese rule in Africa. Married to Portuguse-born, Maria Eugenia da Silva.
Political career: As an *assimilado*, Neto begins work with a number of youth organisations and in 1956 with a group of Angolan workers founded the African Marine Club. Neto gained a medical degree from the University of Lisbon in 1958. From 1959 to 1962, Neto worked as a physician but also wrote poetry denouncing Portuguese rule. This led to his arrest by Portuguese authorities and he was subsequently forced into exile in Cape Verde. After escaping and making his way to Morocco, Neto travelled to Leopoldville (now Kinshasa) where he became involved with the MPLA. Elected leader of the party, Neto travelled to the Soviet Union and Cuba in 1964 to ask for assistance in defeating Portugal. On the independence of Angola (11 November 1975), Neto became the country's first president.
Date of death: 10 September 1979.

MPLA leader Agostinho Neto was excluded from the meeting due to mistrust of his links to the Soviet Union. (angop.ao)

founded in October 1955, or the People's Movement for the Liberation of Angola (MPLA) founded on 10 December 1956. The creation of the MPLA resulted from a merger between the PLUA and the PCA, and other groups such as the Movement for the National Independence of Angola (MINA) and the Democratic Front for the Liberation of Angola (FDLA) later rallied to the MPLA's cause. With its members drawn from the ranks of Luanda's *mestico*, *assimilados* and white Angolan intellectuals, the MPLA's first president was Mario Andrade,[5] who had also been a founding member of the PCA. One objective of the MPLA being to oppose Portuguese rule through political and armed conflict, its programme of social reform meant that it formed close links with other radical political parties in Portuguese colonies. For example, the African Party for the Independence of Guinea and Cape

Jonas Malheiro Savimbi

Date and place of birth: 3 August 1934 in Munhango
Heritage: Ovimbundu
Family: Savimbi's father was Lote Savimbi, a station master and Evangelist preacher. Savimbi was reported to have had several wives and at least 25 children.
Education: Attended Protestant and Catholic schools. Aged 24, he finished secondary schooling in Portugal and met Angolan students preparing political action against the Portuguese government. Savimbi is forced to move from Portugal to Switzerland where he obtains a scholarship to study at the University of Fribourg. Transfers to the University of Lausanne to study Political Science and Law and graduates in 1965.
Political activity: Encouraged by Jomo Kenyatta, in 1961, Savimbi interrupted his studies to become Secretary General of the Union of the Peoples of Angola (UPA), later the FNLA. Forms UNITA in 1966 in Angola's Moxico Province and spends the next eight years leading the party in order to obtain independence. In 1974, UNITA signed agreements with the MPLA and FNLA but by November 1975 all three were fighting a civil war. In February 1976, Savimbi convened the Cuanza River Conference that issued the Cuanza River Manifesto. The objective of the manifesto being to rid Angola of Cuban and Soviet forces in May 1991, Savimbi and Angolan President Jose Eduardo dos Santos signed the Bicesse Accords. This agreement made the way for multi-party elections to be held in September 1992. Renewed civil war broke out in 1993 but Savimbi and the Angolan government signed the Lusaka Protocol in November 1994. The protocol led to the Angolan national army and UNITA forces merging and led to the establishment of the Government of Unity and Reconciliation.
Death: After surviving countless attempts on his life, Savimbi was killed in a battle with government troops on 22 February 2002.

UNITA leader Jonas Savimbi was once a political ally of Holden Roberto. (Author's collection)

Verde (PAIGC), the Mozambique Liberation Front (FRELIMO), and the Movement for the Liberation of São Tomé and Principe (MLSTP). Despite later becoming Angola's largest party and its supplying Angola's first president, Agostinho Neto, in the late 1950s, the MPLA remained a relatively small propaganda group with activities carried out by a few clandestine cells situated within Angola. These activities repressed by the Portuguese security forces, the MPLA only became a major nationalist movement when it established a support base among the Mbundu or Ambundu people.

Around the same time as the MPLA was created, Angola saw the emergence of a second movement, the National Front for the Liberation of Angola (FNLA). Founded in 1954 as the Union of Peoples of Northern Angola (UPNA), in 1959 this movement became the United Peoples of Angola (UPA) before transmuting into the FNLA in 1961. Unlike the MPLA, the UPA – headed by Holden Roberto – was tribally-based and linked to a wider movement aiming for the reestablishment of the 16th century Bakongo kingdom. As such, it had close ties with the party of future Congo-Léopoldville president Joseph Kasa-Vubu, the Alliance of Bakongo (ABAKO) founded in 1955, but similarly to the MPLA, the UPA was opposed to Portuguese rule. Though finding its support primarily in Angola's northern regions, it also had a degree of support in Luanda, among the Mbundu in the cotton growing region of Malanje, and members of the Ovimbundu and Chokwe tribes of central and eastern Angola.

The Angolan Revolution

With political tensions between the Portuguese authorities and Angolan movements gradually increasing, things finally came to a head at the beginning of 1961. Portuguese forces massacred at least 5,000 people on 3-4 January of that year,[6] the MPLA carried out attacks on police stations and prisons in order to free political prisoners, in retaliation Portuguese settlers then attacked villages killing local populations, and on 15 March 1961 in the Bakongo region of northern Angola Portuguese settlements were attacked in planned raids carried out by the UPA. By nightfall, up to a thousand white Angolans including women and young children had been slaughtered.[7] This leading to an outcry in Portugal, Portuguese security forces responded by bombing the regions of Icolo e Bengo and Baixa de Cassanje killing up to 20,000. It has been estimated that in the first eight months of 1961 up to 50,000 people lost their lives to violence,[8] including around 400 Europeans.[9] Despite endeavours by Salazar's government embarking on a programme designed to reform Angola's economy, by the summer of 1961 rebel groups had become more organised militarily speaking. The UPA formed the National Liberation Front of Angola (ELNA), a force of about 5,000 mainly Bakongo tribesmen, and these forces were supported and trained by Algerian National Liberation Front (FNL) forces in Tunisia and Morocco. This was at a time when the FNL was still fighting its own colonial war against France.

In March 1962, the UPA formed an alliance with the Democratic Party of Angola (PDA) to form the National Liberation Front of Angola (FNLA). Basing itself in Congo-Léopoldville, the FNLA then declared that it was the Revolutionary Government of Angola in Exile (GRAE) and that it was the only legitimate authority in Angola. Meanwhile, the MPLA also began to strengthen its political character. This was assisted by the arrival of Agostinho Neto as head of the movement in 1962, and also by its moving from Leopoldville to Brazzaville in the now Republic of the Congo in 1963. This became possible only after the overthrow of Fulbert Youlou, the Roman Catholic priest who became Congo-Brazzaville's first president, and his replacement by Alphonse Massamba-Débat. The latter led the National Movement of the Revolution (MNR), and a follower of the Marxist-inspired Scientific Socialism.

The Congo-Brazzaville's proximity to the Angolan enclave of Cabinda meant that the MPLA focused its guerrilla activities

The Carnation Revolution began on 24 April 1974 against the Estado Novo regime. (TASS)

Here a member of the public discusses events with a soldier of the Portuguese Army. (Author's collection)

The actions of the army were supported by residents of Lisbon who joined soldiers in celebration. (Author's collection)

Marcelo Caetano, Prime Minister of Portugal 1968-1974. (Author's collection)

General Antonio de Spínola replaced Caetano. Spínola was formerly the commander of Portuguese forces in Portuguese Guinea, now Guinea-Bissau. (Author's collection)

on this area. Here, it led several successful operations against the Portuguese in the 1960s, but by the end of the decade it had failed to make any real headway so it switched its attention to eastern Angola. This had been made possible through political affiliations the MPLA made with Zambia and Tanzania, two countries that facilitated the transfer of Chinese and Soviet weapons to Neto's forces. Support such as this meant that the MPLA was gradually able to take over the mantle of the most powerful challenger to Portuguese colonial rule. After it moved its headquarters from Brazzaville to Lusaka in 1968, the following year the MPLA carried out significant operations in Angola's Moxico, Lunda, Bié and Cuando Cubango provinces. By the time the MPLA became Angola's dominant political force, a third movement committed to ending Portuguese rule in Angola had been created. Named the National Union for the Total Independence of Angola (UNITA), it was led by Jonas Savimbi, the former Foreign Minister of the GRAE.

In early July 1964, Savimbi resigned his position due to disputes over policy and was to make immediate contact with China in order to gain political support. He made contact with the Xinhua news agency in Accra, Ghana later that month, and in July and August 1964 he took lessons at the Nanjing Military Academy returning once more in January 1965. The academy was the main guerrilla training institute in China.[10]

The Maoist theories on warfare acquired in China enabled Savimbi to set himself up as the representative of Angola's impoverished, illiterate peasant populations and, as a consequence, UNITA gained a good deal of popularity among the southern Ovimbundu, Chokwe and Ngangela peoples. Militarily small in size, UNITA, however, had little effect on the course of the Angolan War of Independence: once it endeavoured to extend its influence centres beyond its Bié heartlands, UNITA would run into the MPLA which was making its way eastwards. Nevertheless, on the eve of Angolan independence, UNITA could claim the allegiance of around 40 percent of its population making it a formidable ally for any internal or external force.

The Carnation Revolution

The Carnation Revolution of 25 April 1974 came as somewhat of a relief for Marcelo Caetano's beleaguered Portuguese government. In 1973, Portugal's economy was pretty much typical of a group of nations referred to as newly industrialised nations (NICs) that had witnessed rapid economic growth in the 1960s. It remained a relatively poor country, however, and the country's economic situation was to change dramatically when the Organisation of Arab Petroleum Exporting Countries (OAPEC) placed an embargo on nations it believed had supported Israel during the Yom Kippur War. While the embargo initially targeted the United States in retaliation for its decision to supply the Israeli military with oil and thus gain leverage in post-war peace negotiations, it was then extended to the Netherlands, Portugal and South Africa.[11] With Portugal relying on oil for 85 percent of its energy needs, the effect of the embargo was that within the space of just a few months, the rate of inflation in Portugal shot up to over 25 percent on an annual basis.[12] Some of the consequences were that there was a shortage of some food stuffs in Lisbon, and that a wave of strikes that had begun in 1971 accelerated so steadily that on 25 April 1974, a cabinet meeting was due to take place to discuss the threat of the first ever strike by civil servants. In the end, this meeting was never held as Caetano's government was overthrown by the Armed Forces Movement (MFA). Comprised of military officers and politicians such as Vitor Alves, Otelo Saraiva de Carvalho, the MFA had grown increasingly angry with Caetano's decision-making in regards to Portugal's military policy in its colonies. Having already surrendered Goa, Daman and Diu to the Indian Army in December 1961, army commanders believed that government plans to maintain Portugal's remaining overseas possessions by force as unrealistic. There were complaints about a lack of material, the negative treatment given to Portugal's armed forces after the loss of the country's territories in India and, in the colonies, there were complaints about the large difference between the salaries of the military and those of the white settlers.[13] When conflict broke out in Angola in February 1961, even more pressure was piled on to these military forces. Portugal's continuing refusal to cede its African territories and grant them independence led to it becoming isolated on the international stage, and to compound the military situation several nations including the United States and Great Britain imposed arms embargoes on Portugal (and South Africa) meaning that Portuguese forces were denied some of the means of fighting wars in Angola, Portuguese Guinea and Mozambique. The Angolan War of Independence beginning on 4 February 1961, an unprepared Portuguese government rapidly

The name of the revolution takes its name from the flowers given to soldiers or placed in their rifles. (en. somosmascuba.com)

Celebrations began in the morning after the overthrow of Caetano and lasted for several days. (Henrique Matos)

The revolution came as a relief for Portuguese soldiers as well as the general public. (Konflictcam)

found itself confronted by a situation that saw administrative posts in three districts of northern Angola either wiped out or controlled by nationalist groups; over a thousand Portuguese dead along with countless Angolans; the economy crippled and communications damaged or out of action; plus thousands of Portuguese refugees in Luanda or making their way back to Portugal.[14] This resulted in Portugal sending what military supplies it had to support the military and massively increasing the number of Portuguese troops already present. By 1967-1968, it has been estimated that the strength of the army in Angola had increased to around 50,000 – some 15-16 times more than in early 1961[15] – and that the war against African nationalists (in all three wars) was costing Portugal around $300,000 per day. In 1968, military expenditure represented about 50 percent of the total of Portugal's annual budget.[16] Though the end of Portugal's *Estado Novo* regime also came as a relief for Angolans, little did they realise that this meant an end to conflict.

On the morning of 25 April 1974, General Antonio de Spínola emerged as the head of the National Salvation Junta (JSN) and was given the task of governing Portugal during the transitional period. Spínola, himself, had been at the root of the Carnation Revolution as he had been dismissed as Deputy Head of the Joint Chiefs of Staff of the Army. This dismissal came after Spínola published a book entitled *Portugal and the Future* in which he challenged Portuguese policy of using a military rather than a political solution to its colonial wars.[17] Subsequently finding himself in a position whereby he was able to put forward this political solution in being appointed President in mid-May 1974, Spínola set the course for the independence of Portugal's African colonies on 27 July 1974 when he recognised the rights of their peoples to self-determination. By then, however, Spínola's idea that a referendum on Angolan independence be held only after a ceasefire generated opposition from within the MFA and in Angola. Indeed, Portuguese soldiers were still being killed and Angola's three main movements, the People's Movement for the Liberation of Angola (MPLA), the National Liberation Front of Angola (FNLA), and the National Union for the Total Independence of Angola (UNITA), demanded that Portugal affirm its commitment to granting independence before a not after a ceasefire.[18] In a political context worsened by strikes and rioting in the Angolan capital Luanda, Spínola then attempted to influence the path Angola would take towards independence by setting up a meeting in the Cape Verde Islands attended by Zairian president Mobutu Sese Soko, the FNLA's Holden Roberto, Jonas Savimbi of the UNITA, and Daniel Chipenda, the leader of the MPLA's eastern faction and a rival of MPLA leader Agostinho Neto.[19] Taking place on the 14 September 1974, and excluding Neto, Spínola proposed the setting up of a provisional coalition government that would include the Angolan leaders present as well as representatives of tribal, white and coloured minority groups.[20] Ultimately, Spínola's plans came to nothing as the MFA forced his resignation on 30 September 1974. The leaders of this movement saw immediate withdrawal from Angola as the best solution.

From Alvor to civil war

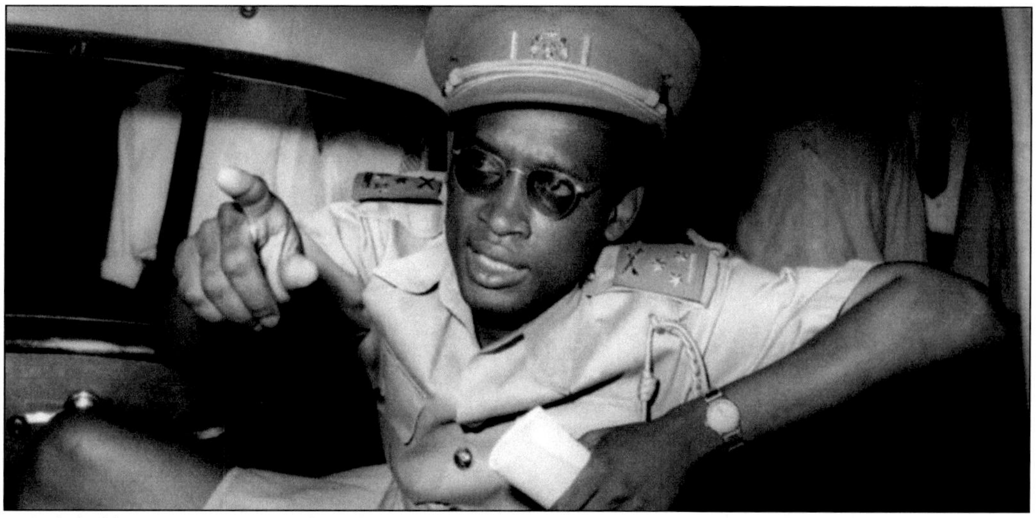

Spínola held a secret meeting with Mobutu Sese Seko, Holden Roberto, Daniel Chipenda and Jonas Savimbi in September 1974. The objective was to set up an Angolan regime headed by representatives of the FNLA, the MPLA and UNITA. Mobutu was Chief of Staff of the Congolese National Army. (Foreign Policy)

Meetings to discuss the terms of Angola's independence were held at Alvor, a coastal town in southern Portugal. (Diario de Noticias)

With Portuguese Guinea gaining its independence on 10 September 1974, and with Spínola replaced by Francisco da Costa Gomes at the end of that month, no sooner had a ceasefire been negotiated than the three main political movements began to jostle for position in a battle that would lead to civil war just a few months later. Divisions between the three movements began with an internal split in the MPLA in September 1974 and came only a few days before the meeting with Spínola in Cape Verde. Problems arose as Agostinho Neto and Daniel Chipenda met in Congo-Brazzaville along with Mario de Andrade[21] to discuss the question of who would lead the MPLA towards independence. These negotiations resulted in a situation whereby Neto would become president of the party while Chipenda and Joaquin de Andrade (Mario's brother) would serve as co-vice presidents.

In the meantime, both Portugal and the Organisation of African Unity (OAU) had been working behind the scenes to bring the three main movements together. In November, Portuguese Foreign Minister Mario Soares brought together the FNLA and UNITA, then a subsequent agreement was reached between UNITA and the MPLA in December 1974. If a step in the right direction, supporters of the FNLA and the MPLA then demonstrated through violent clashes with each other in Luanda that there remained many differences between the two parties. These differences appeared to have been resolved on 3 January 1975 after Kenyan president Jomo Kenyatta organised a conference in Mombasa and hosted the leaders of the three movements. Kenyatta calling for Neto, Savimbi and Roberto to overcome their differences "in the name of mother Africa", and for the sake of the Angolan people, two days later Kenyatta announced that agreement had been reached and that a united front would be formed to negotiate the terms of independence with Portugal at Alvor on 10 January.[22] Held over five days in a small village on Portugal's southern coast, the Alvor Agreement signed on 15 January 1975 granted Angola

The meetings took place from 10-15 January 1975 and ended in the signing of the Alvor Agreement. (Author's collection)

Spínola was replaced by General Francisco da Costa in September 1974. (Author's collection)

Thousands of Portuguese nationals decided to flee Angola after the Alvor Agreement declared Portugal's withdrawal from one of its last African colonies. (Author's collection)

The Mikoyan-Gurevich MiG-17F was a high-subsonic fighter aircraft first produced in 1953. As well as being used in the Angolan Civil War, as many as 36 MiG-17s were used in the Nigerian Civil War (1967-1970). In late 1975, Moscow sold 10 such fighter-bombers to Angola, together with one MiG-15UTI two-seat conversion trainer. (Tom Cooper Collection)

The Antonov An-12 is a four-engined turboprop transport aircraft produced between 1957-1973. The An-12 has capacity for up to 100 fully equipped paratroopers or 20,000 kg of cargo.

The KhMDB T-34/85 was a Soviet medium tank developed during the later stages of the Second World War. This example was photographed on the streets of Luanda in November 1975.

The Mikoyan-Gurevich MiG-21 was a supersonic jet fighter introduced into service in 1959. It was a rare sight in African wars but as well as reportedly being used in Angola it could be found in Somalia and Uganda. All examples delivered to Angola were purchased by the MPLA and flown by Cubans.

The An-22 is a heavy military transport aircraft first used by the Soviet Air Force in 1967. It remains the world's largest turboprop aircraft and is still in service. This An-22 is pictured at Antonov Airport in the Ukraine.

This Aeroflot An-12 was pictured at Luanda Internation, with a group of Cubans in front.

This An-22 was pictured unloading a Ural truck with BM-21 multiple rocket launcher at Luanda International.

Russian military advisors could also be found in Angola, even if their influence was minimal, early on. This group arrived in November 1975 after Angola's independence.

independence from Portugal on 11 November of that year thereby drawing an end to a colonial war that had lasted 13 years. The agreement provided for the creation of a transitional government presided by a Portuguese High Commissioner and a Presidential Committee comprising a representative from each of the three main movements. Supposedly leading to a peaceable transition of power from coloniser to colonised, the months between February and November nonetheless witnessed an escalation of underlying ancient and predominantly tribal rivalries. Punctuated by violent clashes that saw hundreds killed,[23] this period also saw a continuation of an external intervention in Angola that had started as early as 1961 for the Soviet Union, and as early as 1963 for

An MPLA soldier in Luso, July 1975. UNITA declared war on the MPLA following its advances into Ovimbundu territory

An MPLA soldier carrying a (broken) Heckler & Koch G3/CETME. Oftentimes these weapons would be deprived of their stocks through misuse or the lack of means to repair them. The headgear is the standard Soviet Army M52 helmet.

The PPSh 41 was a Soviet sub-machine gun frequently used by the MPLA. Loaded with either a box or drum magazine, the PPSh fired the Tokarev 7.62x25mm round.

These MPLA female recruits were equipped with the G3/CETME.

The Czech-made PLDvK vzor 53 was a towed twin-barreled 30mm anti-aircraft gun, as used on the M53/59 Praga.

Whereas the first MPLA soldier carries a PPSh 41, the second is armed with an SKS semi-automatic carbine chambered for a 7.62x39mm round. Note the Egyptian lizard camouflage worn by these troops. Egypt was a major hub for nationalist movements and acted as a transfer point for Soviet weapons and equipment into Africa.

MPLA troops with ammunition captured from the FNLA. Note the USAID markings on the cases. This photo was taken in Caxito in December 1975.

The MPLA used any headgear that was available.

Cuba.[24] The Soviet Union's assistance to the MPLA consisting of what it termed as "political and practical guidance",[25] in reality this was the supply of around 131 million dollars' worth of equipment up to March 1975.[26] This included arms shipments in August and October 1974, and by January 1975 the Soviet Union had delivered enough weapons to arm 5-7,000 MPLA combatants.[27] In December 1974, it then equipped the MPLA's armed wing, the Popular Armed Forces for the Liberation of Angola (FAPLA) with heavy weapons and ammunition.[28] Whereas previous shipments had arrived in Dar Es Salaam, as reported by the Tanzanian press,[29] later supplies arrived in Angola via the Republic of the Congo, a major transit point during the Angolan conflict. From March 1975 to January 1976 alone, the Soviet Union then delivered equipment with a value of some $100-200 million.[30] This came in the shape of MiG-17 and possibly MiG-21 fighter aircraft, bridge-building equipment, amphibious vehicles, T-34/85 tanks, 9M14 Malyutka anti-tank missiles, a quantity of BM-13 Katyusha rocket launchers, personnel carriers, and anti-aircraft guns,[31] all transported aboard Antonov An-12 or An-22 cargo planes.

As for the FNLA, which, at the beginning of 1975 allegedly possessed some 21,000 combatants (9,000 in northern Angola and 12,000 in Zaire),[32] from 1973 it had begun to accept arms shipments from the People's Republic of China (PRC),[33] and on 29 May 1974 the first contingent of 112 Chinese military advisors arrived to train FNLA forces.[34] On 28 August 1974, the Romanian press announced that the country's communist party had delivered a large amount of military equipment to Roberto's forces,[35] and on 10 September Holden announced that the FNLA

Jonas Savimbi pictured with Commandant S.W.J. (Willie) Kotzé, the Second-in-Command of Task Force Zulu during Operation Savannah.

A UNITA fighter pictured here with a Soviet-made RPD light machine gun. Used in a large number of conflicts since 1944, the RPD fired a 7.62x54mmR round. This one had no doubt been captured from the MPLA.

As well as using weapons captured from the MPLA, UNITA soldiers used the FN FAL. A Belgian-designed rifle, it was standard issue for many North Atlantic Treaty Organisation (NATO) countries and was used by South African and Rhodesian security forces.

A number of UNITA soldiers possessed weapons but no shoes. The UNITA soldier on the left carries an FN FAL 7.62mm battle rifle. Also of note, the SADF pictured here are wearing captured East German helmets.

As with the MPLA, women fighters could be found fighting alongside the men of UNITA.

UNITA forces were mainly composed of peasant populations from the southern and eastern regions of Angola. Generally, they were very poor and had no previous training in how to use weapons.

had received a shipment of 450 tons of military equipment, again from the Chinese.[36]

As violence between the three warring parties continued to rage in Luanda and MPLA members killed around 260 UNITA recruits on 4 June 1975,[37] from June 15-21 June 1975 Jomo Kenyatta once again acted as a mediator in the conflict when hosting a meeting of the three Angolan leaders in Nakuru, Kenya. Despite the subsequent Nakuru Agreement initiating a truce, it was only a matter of time before fighting broke out once again in the Angolan capital. This time, on 2 July, the MPLA killed hundreds of UNITA supporters as they fled Luanda and made their way across the Cuanza River to the central highlands.[38] The FAPLA and the *Poder Popular* (an MPLA militia) then expelled remaining

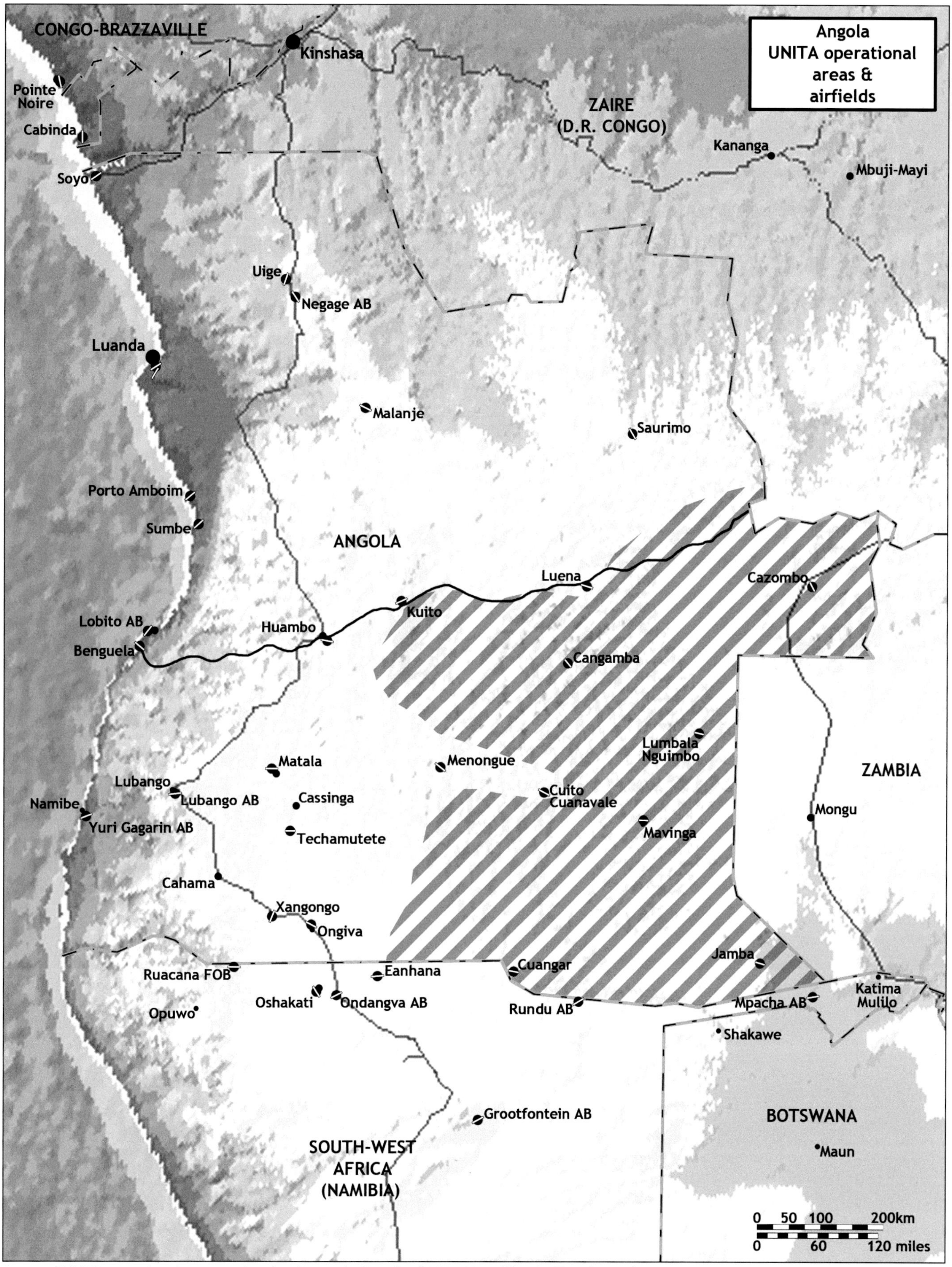

A map of UNITA operational areas, and major airports in Angola of 1975-1976. (Map by Tom Cooper)

Here UNITA recruits receive training on a light machine gun.

A pair of AML-90s operated by the CIA-recruited mercenaries: the vehicles in question were of French design and manufacture and originally sold to Congo/Zaire. The almost identical Eland-90 armoured car was built for the SADF to carry out long-range reconnaissance.

The remains of a FAPLA convoy destroyed during Operation Savannah.

Typically, the Eland-90 was fitted with M1919 Browning 7.62mm machine guns (with 2,440 – 3,800 rounds). Its main armament was a 90mm Denel GT-2 cannon with 29 rounds, as seen here. Other variants of the Eland were armed with a 60mm breach-loading gun-mortar or a 20mm cannon.

The 5.5-inch G2 Howitzer was one of the field guns used by the SADF during Operation Savannah.

FNLA and UNITA supporters from Luanda in an offensive that cost 3,000 lives,[39] and with fighting over the past five months or so having led to the deaths of some 40,000, the MPLA controlled the Lunda Sul and Lunda Norte provinces, as well as areas around the Atlantic coastal cities of Lobito, Benguela and Moçâmedes.

The advances into these traditional Ovimbundu territories and later advances into the UNITA stronghold of Luso (now Luena) resulted in UNITA formally declaring war on the MPLA on 1 August. Furthermore, they would play a decisive role in shaping the course of the Angolan Civil War as they sparked the arrival of two more foreign forces into the conflict, South Africa and Cuba.

South African Intervention, 1975

As part of a strategy against a loose coalition of African states committed to ending apartheid and known as the Frontline States (FLS),[40] since the mid-1960s the South African Defence Force (SADF) had been deployed to areas in which potential threats to the South African regime had been identified. One particular case was South West Africa (now Namibia) which came under South African administration in 1915 and which, since 1960, had seen an increase in guerrilla activities carried out by two organisations both backed by the FLS, the South West Africa People's Organisation (SWAPO) and the South West Africa National Union (SWANU). Though SWAPO had emerged as the dominant organisation of the two by the early 1960s, it was not until 26 August 1966 that it made its first attack against South African security forces. This occurred when SWAPO forces clashed with a unit of the South African police at Omugulugwombashe in northern Namibia.[41]

Over the next 24 years, the SADF implemented a number of strategies intended to protect Namibia's, and its own, borders from infiltration by SWAPO's armed wing, the South West Africa Liberation Army (SWALA). This included extending its operational areas into Angola and fighting alongside Portuguese forces as they battled against those seeking independence. For example, the SADF jointly operated an air command post at Cuito Cuanavale in southern Angola, and it provided aircraft and troops for COIN operations.[42]

Portugal's decision to withdraw from Angola came as a blow to a strategy that kept the activities of the SWALA/PLAN to a minimum.[43] Not only did this withdrawal mean the disappearance of a buffer state between South Africa and the forces of the FLS, Pretoria also feared that the replacement of a virulent anti-communist regime with one that was sympathetic to this ideology opened the way for the PLAN to set up bases in Angola. From here, PLAN forces could pass over the border into Namibia. While this matter remained theoretical in the aftermath of the Carnation Revolution, as the civil war began in earnest in the summer of 1975, Pretoria grew concerned about more practical questions. South Africa had recently invested massively in a hydroelectric power plant on the Cunene River that served northern Namibia's energy needs, and it feared that control of the plant would be lost to unfriendly forces if no action was taken. Consequently, in early August, a 30-man contingent of SADF troops was sent to fend off potential attack.

By late August 1975, Pretoria had begun to implement measures to provide support to anti-MPLA forces. Representatives of the SADF Military Intelligence and those of the Bureau of State Security (BOSS) had held frequent meetings with Chipenda and Savimbi from April 1975, and this resulted in Prime Minister John Vorster asking they draw up a report evaluating the outcome of the Angolan Civil War as it stood. The report given to Vorster on 26 June concluding that the war would end in victory for the MPLA, on 14 July Vorster authorised the transfer of 20 million rand ($14 million) of weapons to the FNLA and UNITA.[44] In September, at a time when it was decided that the SADF would provide training and logistical support to Chipenda's forces based in M'Pupa in the Cuanda Cubango region,[45] and to Savimbi's forces at Calombo near Silva Porto (now Cuito) in central Angola.

In order to provide the training and to constitute forces capable of stemming the advance of the FAPLA, by early October the SADF had appointed a number of its senior officers to set up Combat Groups. Task Force Zulu was the main force and comprised Alpha and Bravo CGs. Commanded by Commandant Dellville Lindford, Alpha was made of indigenous Flecha commandos, a company of Bushman, while Bravo under the command of Jan Breytenbach included Chipenda's former FNLA soldiers. Other CGs (Foxbat, Orange, and X-Ray) were commanded by Commandant Eddie Webb, Commandant Dolf Carstens and Captain Fred Rindel respectively. Contrary to Task Force Zulu, the forces composing Orange and X-Ray included regular SADF

Cuban aid to the MPLA dated back to the early 1960s. In this photo we see Fidel Castro in the company of Agostinho Neto. (Cuba Si)

The Cuban advisors to the MPLA/FAPLA were organised into the Cuban Military Mission in Angola (*Misión Militar de Cuba en Angola*, MMCA). The MMCA was initially headed by Commandante Raúl Díaz Argüelles (sunglasses). Argüelles was a veteran of war in Guinea-Bissau and was killed in Angola on 11 December 1975. (Author's collection).

forces (B Company of the South African Infantry Battalion) and a company of the Zairian Army.

Though there were a number of skirmishes with the FAPLA in early October, the start of Operation Savannah on 14 October signalled the beginning of the South African commanded offensive to push back enemy forces and to regain control of strategically important industrial infrastructures. Zones around the Benguela Railway were taken within a matter of days, and subsequent victories at Pereira d'Eça (N'Giva), Sá da Bandeira (Lubango), Evale, João de Ameida (Chibia) and Rotunda meant that Task Force Zulu took Moçâmedes, Angola's southernmost port, on 28 October. Whereas CG Foxtrot had meanwhile set up positions around Nova Lisboa (Huambo) to the southeast of Luanda, it was not yet clear whether the final objective consisted in reaching the capital before the independence of Angola due to be proclaimed just two weeks later. Given the weak resistance its forces had faced Pretoria was confident that Task Force Zulu would be capable of gaining more ground in a short space of time, but at that point it had not decided how far north its forces should go. This indecision proved to be fatal as it gave FAPLA the time to regroup. Moreover, it began to receive larger quantities of arms and increasing support from professional soldiers in the shape of Cubans.

Cuban Intervention, 1975

As indicated earlier in this chapter, the MPLA's connection to Castro's Cuba dates back to the early 1960s, or as early as the late 1950s if meetings between students at the Casa dos Estudantes do Império in Lisbon are taken into account. Here, students from Lusophone Africa would redesign the shape of the world through revolutionary discussion, and it was through this Imperial Student House that the MPLA made its first contacts with Castro's 26 July Movement.[46] After Castro's regime overthrew Fulgencio Batista in January 1959, Havana became the centre for a series of subversive operations in any number of Latin American countries for which Cuba provided weapons, training and, sometimes, its own military personnel. Nor was this type of activity limited simply to countries within Central and South America. As liberation movements were created or expanded in the late 1950s and early 1960s, Cuba sought to establish links with organisations set up to combat colonial presence in Portuguese Guinea, Mozambique, Rhodesia and Ethiopia. Direct Cuban intervention started in June 1959 when Guevara and Raúl Castro travelled to Cairo, and it continued after Fidel Castro castigated France in September 1960 over its war in Algeria, and promised Cuba's support for the Algerian people, the "remaining colonial peoples in Africa" and the "Negroes who are discriminated against in the Union of South Africa".[47] From December 1961, Cuba began supplying weapons to Algeria's National Liberation Front (FLN): in that month, the *Bahia de Nipe*,

In November 1975 the Cuban armed forces initiated the Operation Carlota, a military intervention in Angola, which brought complete units of the FAR to Angola. This photograph shows regular troops of the Cuban Army in front of a BM-21 multiple rocket launcher: a weapon that was to play a crucial role during all major battles of late 1975 and early 1976.

a Cuban vessel, left Havana and transported its cargo of 1,500 rifles, more than 30 machine guns, four US-made 81mm mortars and a large quantity of US-made mortar rounds.[48] These weapons and ammunition had been captured from Brigade 2506 at the Bay of Pigs.[49] In addition to its support for Algeria, in 1961 Cuba allegedly supplied weapons to rebel movements in Zanzibar in 1961, and from early 1964 Cuban military personnel accompanied Algerian weapons shipments to Tanzania. Cuba also sent shiploads of weapons including tanks to Algeria during its brief conflict with Morocco in October 1963.[50]

A more direct Cuban approach to Africa's wars came about towards the end of 1964 when Ernesto Guevara left Havana and began a goodwill tour as Castro's emissary. One of Guevara's first ports of call was New York where he addressed dignitaries attending the 19th General Assembly of the United Nations on 11 December, but by early January 1965 he had made his way across the Atlantic and found himself in Congo-Brazaville for discussions with Alphonse Massamba-Débat. With the MPLA also being based in Brazaville, on 5 January Guevara met a number of the party's leading officials including Political Secretary, Lucio Lara and Foreign Secretary, Luis de Azevedo.

The Cuban merchant *La Plata* arrived at Pointe-Noire in the Republic of the Congo in October 1975. It carried troops and materials in support of MPLA operations in Cabinda. (Author's collection)

At a time when Guevara had his mind fixed on sending Cubans to train Laurent-Desiré Kabila's forces in the east of neighbouring Democratic Republic of the Congo, and on starting his pan-African revolution, his suggestion that Neto send his troops to the Congo for similar training was not well received. The MPLA had lost political ground to the rival FNLA since its expulsion from Leopoldville in 1963, and in Cabinda where the MPLA had centred its guerrilla activity against Portuguese forces the MPLA was making no headway. What Neto needed was for Cuba to send instructors so that they could train MPLA soldiers to carry out operations in northern Angola (the MPLA's 1st Military Region) and in Cabinda (2nd Military Region).[51] This would have the effect of countering increasing popular support for the FNLA and bolstering support for the MPLA in the Cabinda enclave.

Nicknamed "Stalin's Organ", there were many variants of Soviet-made multiple rocket launchers – a formidable weapon first used by the USSR in 1939. The version deployed in Angola was the BM-21, this had a total of 40 tubes for 122mm rockets. (Author's collection)

Though Guevara moved on to the Afro-Asian Conference in Algiers then to the Congo in April 1965, just three weeks after Neto's meeting with Guevara, Cuban Revolutionary Force (FAR) commander Victor Dreke received an order from the Cuban Army High Command to start the recruitment of men for an assignment which could last for a period of up to two years.[52] Not yet aware of where the mission would take place, Dreke nonetheless selected a group of 500 men to join him and began their training at the Piti 1 Camp in Pinar del Rio. At some point during the next two months with Dreke's forces now divided into two separate units, it was decided that the first, Columna 1 (or the Lumumba

One of the Cuban commanders was General Rafael Moracen. Here (centre), he is pictured in an Angolan village just outside Luanda.

Soviet equipment used by Cuban forces included the six-wheeled BTR-152. An Armoured Personnel Carrier (APC), the BTR-152 could be equipped with a 7.62mm SG-43 Goryunov medium machine gun (1,250 rounds) or a DShK Heavy machine gun (500 rounds), but this example has a US-made Browning M1919.

Another Soviet vehicle used by Cuban forces in Angola was the GAZ-66. This one was disabled by the SADF during Operation Savannah and captured at Bridge 14 in December 1975.

Battalion) would be assigned to the Democratic Republic of the Congo while the second, Columna 2, was to travel to Brazzaville. Though the intervention of Cuban troops in Cabinda was to mark the beginning of a 26-year alliance with the MPLA, Cuba's initial efforts in Angola were inauspicious due to the difficult terrain found in the Mayombe jungle, and the lack of support from local tribes more likely to support the Front for the Liberation of the Enclave of Cabinda (FLEC) than the Mbundu-dominated MPLA. Cuban forces subsequently withdrew from Cabinda at the end of 1965 while Cuba turned its focus to Latin America.

Though Cubans could be found fighting alongside the PAIGC in Guinea-Bissau until the Carnation Revolution, it was not until the summer of 1975 that they returned to Central Africa. Resulting from appeals made by Neto for help in training the FAPLA, in July Neto met with representatives of the Cuban Military Mission in Angola (MMCA), a delegation of army officers headed by Commandante Raúl Díaz Argüelles, a veteran of the campaign in Guinea-Bissau. On his return to Havana in early August, Díaz Argüelles recommended that Castro send a group of around 90 Cuban Revolutionary Armed Forces (FAR) officers and NCOs to Angola in order to set up training centres for the FAPLA known as *Centros de Instrucción Revolucionaria* (CIR). This number increasing to nearly 500 by the end of the month, nearly 200 Cubans were sent to Cabinda while four other groups were sent to Henrique de Carvalho (now Saurimo) in the Lunda Sul Province, to an area south of the Benguela Railway to protect the main route from southern Angola, and to Salazar (now N'dalatando) in the province of Cuanza Norte.

The first group of Cubans arrived in Cabinda at the end of September, and on 5 October the Cuban supply ship *Vietnam Heroico* unloaded its cargo of troops and material at Porto Amboim in the Cuanza Sul province. Four days later, *La Plata* arrived at Pointe-Noire in the Republic of the Congo carrying men and supplies for Cabinda. These arrivals signalling the beginning of Operation Carlota, Cuba's priority was to help the MPLA keep hold of Luanda.

3
United States Involvement in the Angolan Civil War

If the Angolan Civil War were viewed through a wide optic then US involvement can be explained through a commitment to a series of policies developed from 1947. The overall aim of these policies being to ensure that nations were free from coercion,[1] they joined concepts such as the Domino Theory. First expounded in the early 1950s, the tenets of this theory were that should a given nation's political decisions be influenced by communist doctrine then there was a risk that its neighbours would follow suit. Eventually, whole regions would be dominated by Soviet ideology leaving the United States without access to areas deemed important for strategic, economic or political reasons. On the basis that the United States could not intervene militarily in these areas for fear that intervention would spark off a third world war, just after Second World War President Truman's administration implemented a series of measures that provided the tools for covert operations to be carried out in nations identified as being relevant to the objectives of US foreign policy. The National Security Act of 1947 being the most important of these measures, its intention was to restructure the US military and the US intelligence-gathering services. In terms of the military the act led to the creation of the National Military Establishment (NME), the creation of the Department of the Air Force and the creation of the United States Air Force (USAF), and from the point of view of intelligence it led to the creation of the Central Intelligence Agency (CIA). All military and intelligence activities were to be overseen by the National Security Council (NSC).

While overt military operation carried out by the United States in the 1950s included participation in the Korean War (1950-1953) or Operation Blue Bat (1958), from 1948 the CIA could be found operating in Europe (Albania, 1949), in the Pacific (Philippines, 1948-1954) or in the Middle East (Iran, 1953). These operations being limited in scale, much larger CIA covert operations took place in Guatemala in 1954 when it assisted the overthrow of Jacobo Arbenz, and in Cuba when from 1959 the CIA tried to overthrow Fidel Castro of Cuba. The most prominent feature of operations codenamed Mongoose was the failed invasion of Cuba carried out by Cuban exile paramilitary group Brigade 2506 at the Bay of Pigs in April 1961. As far as operations in Africa were concerned, the presence of colonial powers acted as a bulwark against Soviet ambitions. Much was to change with the advent of decolonisation though, and as nations in sub-Saharan Africa became independent the United States realised that it would have to take a far greater interest in the events taking place. Consequently, with the Gold Coast due to become Ghana in March 1957, Vice-President Richard Nixon embarked on a three-week long goodwill visit of a number of newly independent African nations as a show of support, and the following year Eisenhower's administration set up the Bureau of African Affairs with the same goal.

Still considered as somewhat of a "political backwater" by the US State Department,[2] one area of Africa that came to prominence was Congo-Léopoldville. Having gained its independence on 30 June 1960, what concerned US officials was that its prime minister, Patrice Lumumba, appeared to hold communist sympathies. These suspicions confirmed by Lumumba's appeal to the Soviet Union for assistance in putting an end to the presence of Belgian troops and to the secession of two of the Congo's provinces.[3] Lumumba's doing so led to accusations that he was a "stalking horse for what appeared to be a Soviet effort to take over the Congo",[4] and with this conclusion his fate was sealed. Armée Nationale Congolaise (ANC) Chief of Staff Joseph Mobutu then organised a coup d'état along with help from the CIA, and the United States then spent the next seven years ensuring that radical socialism could not gain a foothold in Central Africa. The means it employed included constituting clandestine air and naval forces made up principally of Cuban exiles while, at the same time it propped up successive pro-Western governments through the provision of financial and advisory assistance.[5] From 1967, the year in which the so-called 'Congo Crisis' came to an end, the United States was safe in the knowledge that it had a friend in Mobutu. As we shall see, United States maintenance of healthy relations with Mobutu was highly beneficial when it came the question of Angola.

The next major changes in US foreign policy appeared when Nixon defeated Hubert Humphrey and George Wallace to become America's 37th President. Following his inauguration in January 1969, Nixon began to pursue two policies that culminated in 1972. The first was the normalisation of relations with the PRC while the second was implementing arms controls and disarmament. Negotiations with the USSR having started in November 1969 and an agreement signed in May 1972, the Strategic Arms Limitation Talks (SALT 1) paved the way for increasing *détente* between the world's two superpowers. One of the most prominent figures involved in the reshaping of US foreign policy during Nixon's presidency was the German-born Henry Kissinger. Nixon's, then Gerald Ford's national security advisor, Kissinger has frequently been credited with introducing a more "realistic" approach to international relations to the White House. "Realpolitik", the idea that political goals should be determined by what was important in a concrete way rather than an abstract one, was behind the decision to ease tensions with communist-bloc countries, and behind a number of decisions taken in regards to Southern Africa.

Insofar as the Southern Africa and US Cold War policy, nations such as the Belgian Congo, Rhodesia and South Africa supplied many of the strategic minerals required for the development of nuclear weapons in the 1940s, the weapons developed in the 1950s and 1960s, as well the means to deliver them. These minerals included a strain of uranium (235) used for the development of bombs dropped on Hiroshima and Nagasaki, and the cobalt, vanadium, chromite, antimony, platinum, magnesium, gold and asbestos used in the fabrication of the superalloys needed for the production of jet fighters and heavy bombers used in long-distance combat operations. The Boeing B-52 Stratofortress, the Lockheed C-130 Hercules, the Boeing KC-135 Stratotanker and the Lockheed U-2 all being examples. In fact, US reliance on Africa's minerals was so great that an entire foreign policy was based on the ability to maintain access to them. With many of the minerals listed found in Rhodesia and South Africa, in 1969 Nixon issued National Security Study Memorandum (NSSM) 39. Otherwise known as the 'Tar Baby' option, NSSM 39 was based on the presumption that colonialism and apartheid were unpleasant realities that for pragmatic reasons should be accommodated.

Timeline of US Involvement in Angola

1947 – The National Security Act of 1947 is a major restructuring of the US military and intelligence agencies. It leads to the creation of the National Security Council (NSC) and the Central Intelligence Agency (CIA) as well as the merger of the Department of War and the Department of the Navy into the National Military Establishment (NME). One of the CIA's earliest actions takes place in France when it arms the Guerini crime family to break strikes initiated by the General Confederation of Labour (CGT), a communist dominated workers' union.
1948 – The Office of Policy Coordination is created. Its responsibilities include carrying out subversive activities against hostile states, assisting clandestine anti-communist resistance groups. In legislative elections held in Italy in 1948, the CIA providing funding for centrist parties and distributed propaganda intended to discredit the Italian Communist Party (PCI).
1949 – The Albanian Subversion was a joint project carried out by the UK's Secret Intelligence Service (SIS) or MI6 and the CIA. The objective was to organise subversive paramilitary activities in Albania in order to inspire a popular uprising against growing Soviet influence in the country.
1951 – The US signs the Azores Agreement with Portugal. It provides the US with military bases in the Azores Islands.
1953 – The CIA orchestrates the overthrow of Iranian Prime Minister Mohammad Mosaddegh. The objective of Operation Ajax is to replace Mosaddegh with Mohammed Reza Pahlavi, the Shah of Iran.
1954 – Operation PB/SUCCESS sees the overthrow of President Jacobo Arbenz of Guatemala and the installation of a military dictatorship led by Carlos Castillo Armas. Arbenz had initiated land reforms, a minimum wage and had been identified by the United States as a communist sympathiser.
1956 – Operation Straggle is a plan to fight against possible communist infiltration of the government in Syria. It is followed by Operation Wappen in 1957, an attempt to eliminate communist influence within the ranks of the Syrian regime.
1957 – Eisenhower orders the CIA to overthrow Indonesia's Sukarno. An attempted coup fails to dislodge him from power.
1959 – The CIA begins a series of attempts to assassinate Fidel Castro of Cuba.
1960 – The CIA is involved in the plot to overthrow the Congo's Patrice Lumumba. The first prime minister of the newly independent country formerly known as the Belgian Congo, Lumumba is identified as being a communist sympathiser. The CIA then sponsors a succession of friendly governments and sponsors Mobutu in a second coup d'Etat that took place in 1965. Mobutu remains in power until 1997.
1961 – The Bay of Pigs invasion of 17 April is an attempt to overthrow Fidel Castro of Cuba. It is followed by Operation Mongoose, a series of attacks against Cuba sponsored by the CIA. The same year, the CIA organises the assassination of Rafael Trujillo, the president of the Dominican Republic, and backs a military force that overthrows President José Velasco of Ecuador.
1963 – The CIA sponsors a successful coup against President Ngo Dinh Diem of South Vietnam.
1963 – The CIA begins to make payments to Holden Roberto in Angola. It does so as the rival MPLA is sponsored by the Soviet Union and Roberto's FNLA/GRAE is an opponent of this party. The United States also sponsors the anti-communist Dr. Eduardo Mondlane in Mozambique. In Ecuador, the CIA sponsors the overthrow of President Arosemana.
1964-1973 – The CIA is implicated in a series of coups in Bolivia, Brazil, Indonesia, Ghana and Chile.
1969 – Richard Nixon and Henry Kissinger adopt the 'Tar Baby' option. Officially known as NSSM 39, it states that the United States will tolerate the existence of white minority regimes due to their strategic and economic importance to US Cold War objectives. The option is reinforced by the Byrd Amendment of 1971, which prohibits the US government from banning the importation from any non-communist country when importations of these minerals from communist countries was permitted.
1970 – The CIA organises the overthrow of Prince Sahounek and replaces him with Lon Nol.
1971 – The Democratic Republic of the Congo (DRC) becomes Zaire.
1972 – Richard Nixon sends a team of burglars to install wire-tapping devices at the Democrat Party's headquarters in Washington D.C.
1973 – The Watergate scandal is exposed by Carl Berstein and Bob Woodward of the *Washington Post*.
1973 – Nixon fires CIA Director Richard Helms and replaces him with William Colby.
1974 – In August, Nixon resigns in light of his implication in the Watergate scandal and he is replaced by Gerald Ford. In December, Seymour Hersh of the *New York Times* publishes an article detailing CIA covert activities over the years. His report leads to the establishment of the Church Committee on 27 January 1975. Its role is to investigate the legality of the CIA's operations.
1975 – In January, the CIA sends $300,000 to Roberto.
In April, the last Americans leave the US Embassy in Saigon.
Ford authorises Operation IA/FEATURE. The objective is to support the FNLA and UNITA in their war against the MPLA in Angola.
John Stockwell is appointed as head of Operation IA/FEATURE at the end of July.
In August, the first shipments of US weapons leave for Angola.
On 11 November Angola becomes an independent nation despite Operation IA/FEATURE and the financial and military involvement of South Africa, Zaire and France.

Another piece of legislation that seemingly gave justification to the US continuing imports from these countries despite UN sanctions was the Byrd Amendment (1971). An amendment to the US Federal Strategic and Critical Minerals Stockpiling Act (1939) also known as the Military Procurement Authorisation (1971), this prohibited the US government from banning the importation of any non-communist country when importations of these minerals from communist countries was permitted. US mining companies were to benefit from this legislation and in 1977 Alcan, Amax, Kennecot, Falconbridge, Foote Minerals and Union Carbide still had subsidiaries in either Rhodesia, South Africa or South West Africa.[6] The amendment also covering trade with Portugal, it enabled Gulf Oil to continue to extract petroleum from sources situated off the coast of Cabinda.[7] In 1966, its subsidiary Cabinda Gulf Oil discovered extensive oil deposits in this region and by the early 1970s it was producing around 10 million tons of oil per year. This made Angola the fourth largest oil producer in the world after Libya, Algeria and Nigeria.[8] Though the largest of foreign oil producers, it was not the

The North American F-86 Sabre first saw service with the USAF in 1948. This photograph shows four examples that entered service with the Portuguese Air Force in the 1950s. Because of pressure from Washington, they saw very brief service in the Guine (Guinea-Bissau) only. (Author's collection)

First entering service in 1941, the Douglas C-47 Skytrain was a feature of many conflicts in Africa and was used by the FAP in Angola, the South African Air Force (SAAF) and the Rhodesian Air Force (RhAF). The civilian version of the C-47 was the DC-3. This example from the Portuguese Air Force was photographed after a landing mishap in the 1960s.

The Douglas C-54 Skymaster was another transport aircraft used by the FAP and supplied by the United States. Making its first flight in 1942, the C-54 was used in the Second World War, the Berlin Airlift (1948-1949), and the Korean War.

The Lockheed Ventura PV-2 Harpoon was first introduced in 1943. Used in ground attacks, the PV-2 was powered by two Pratt & Whitney R-2800-31 air-cooled radial engines. Typically, it was armed with two 0.50 cal machine guns in the upper nose decking as well as two 0.50 cal machine guns in the undernose. A further two machine guns could be placed in the dorsal turret while two others could be found in the rear ventral position. Under the wings, the PV62 could carry eight 5-inch High Velocity Aircraft Rockets (HVARs).

The Lockheed P2V Neptune was first introduced in 1947. A twin-engined long-range maritime patrol and anti-submarine aircraft, it was powered by two Wright R-3350-32 radial engines. In addition to its capability to carry nuclear weapons, the PV-2 was used by the CIA in a number of covert operations in the 1950s and used by the US Navy in Vietnam as a gunship. Later, the P2V was used by the Argentine Naval Aviation (COAN) during the Falklands War.

first. Belgian Petrofina began extraction in 1955 later becoming Petrangol; Occidental, Exxon (US); and Elf (France) all began operations in the 1950s and 1960s, and in the 1970s US-controlled Texaco discovered oil in near Saint Antonio de Zaire (now Soyo) in the northeaster tip of Angola. After coffee, with exports of some $206 million of exports to the United States in 1973,[9] Angolan diamonds came third on the list of the country's riches. With diamond fields also being found mainly in north eastern Angola, in the early 1970s the mining of this mineral was dominated by the Compagnia de Diamantes de Angola (Diamang). Controlled by De Beers Consolidated Mines Ltd., this South African-based company was a subsidiary of the Anglo-American Corporation of South Africa.

Though these commodities represented a non-negligible interest for US industries, economic considerations were somewhat outweighed by US agreements made with Portugal for the use of Lajes Air Base in the Azores. Situated on the island of Terceira, in 1951 Truman's administration signed a deal that would provide American naval and air forces with a stopover point in the mid-Atlantic. These agreements renewed in 1957,[10] Terceira served as a base for US participation in Operation Overlord (1944), Operation Blue Bat (1958), the Berlin Crisis (1961), the Congo Crisis (1960-1967), the October 1973 Arab-Israeli War, and for operations during the First Persian Gulf War (1991). Having become so crucial to the US with over $12 million being spent annually by 1971,[11] both the Kennedy and Eisenhower administrations strengthened ties with Salazar and paid particular attention to happenings taking place in Portuguese colonies that might swing wider aspects of the Cold War in favour of the Soviet Union. Consequently, US policy towards Angola following the uprisings of 1961 consisted of continuing to provide Salazar with extensive military aid and sponsoring Angolan leaders identified as being potentially favourable to US interests should independence be acquired. The military assistance having begun in 1951 on the signing of the Azores Agreement, and the CIA being handed the task of evaluating which leader fitted the bill,[12] the US chose to nurture relations with Holden Roberto that had begun as early as 1955.[13] As Roberto's GRAE was seen as a bulwark to the

The Douglas B-26 Invader was a feature of many of the wars that took place from its introduction in 1942 (designated B-26 from 1948-1965). Typically equipped with 20mm or 37mm auto cannons, six or eight .50 cal machine guns were found in the nose section of the aircraft. Used by a number of different air forces around the world, the B-26 Invader saw service in the Second World War, the Korean War, the Biafran War and the Angolan War of Independence. Notably, the B-26 was used in the Congo by the Congolese Air Force, an air unit composed principally of Cuban exiles. Previously, some of the unit's pilots had flown the B-26 during the Bay of Pigs invasion in April 1961.

The North American T-6 Texan or Harvard was another aircraft supplied by the United States to Portugal. A trainer aircraft that made its first flight in 1938, the T-6 was typically powered by a Pratt & Whitney Wasp R-1340 9-cylinder air-cooled radial engine capable of producing a maximum speed of 320 mph. Other variants of the engine used were the R-1340-47, the R-1340-49, the R-1340-AN-1 or the R-1340-36. Similarly to the B-26, the T-6 saw service in a number of African conflicts, the Algerian War, the Congo Crisis, the Biafran War and wars in Angola and Mozambique being just some examples.

Soviet-backed MPLA, the CIA first offered major assistance to Roberto in March 1962.[14] As for Mozambique, the US chose to support Dr. Eduardo Mondlane, the main figure in the Frente de Libertação de Moçambique (FRELIMO) and did so until the latter's assassination in 1969.

The United States and Mobutu

If a number of different economic and political stakes were at play in Southern Africa, a consideration that influenced US intervention in Angola above almost any other were US relations with Mobutu Sese Soko of Zaire. US dealings with the Zairian president had started as early as mid-1960 when Larry Devlin arrived in the then Congo-Léopoldville to take up the role of the CIA's Chief of Station in a country that had only just gained its independence from Belgium. Congo-Léopoldville presided by Joseph Kasa-Vubu and with Patrice Lumumba as its prime minister, the then Joseph Mobutu was Chief of Staff of the Armée Nationale Congolaise (ANC). Following its independence, Congo-Léopoldville was rapidly overcome by general chaos that triggered the secession of two provinces which subsequently set off a series of internecine political battles and civil warfare. Mobutu played a central role in bringing some semblance of order by colluding with a group of pro-Western politicians known as the Binza Group. The name taken from the wealthy district of Leopoldville (Kinshasa) in which these politicians resided, Mobutu had by then formed cordial relations with Devlin leading to the CIA recognising the Binza Group as an alternative to Lumumba. Indeed, Lumumba's links to radical African leaders such as Ghana's Kwame Nkrumah and his support for the tenets of Pan-Africanism sparked fears in the US State Department that Lumumba was a communist sympathiser. Effectively, pan-Africanist ideology contained elements of socialism and was therefore considered by certain US officials as

Richard Milhous Nixon (b.1913 – d.1994) was the 37th President of the United States, serving from 1969 to 1974. Forced to resign following the Watergate scandal of June 1972, Nixon had formerly served as Vice-President to Dwight D. Eisenhower. (wunc)

German-born Henry Kissinger (b.1923) was the 56th US Secretary of State and served under both Nixon and Ford. A Jewish refugee who fled Nazi Germany in 1938, he was the architect of Operation IA/FEATURE. (NobelPrize.org)

being unfriendly to US objectives in Southern Africa lest it open the way for the Soviet Union to increase its presence in the region thus depriving the United States and its pro-Western allies of access to important stocks of valuable minerals that lie beneath the Congolese soil. Unfortunately for Lumumba, when Katanga and South Kasai seceded in July and August 1960, he ill-advisedly called for assistance from the Soviet Union thereby confirming suspicions that he was a "stalking horse for what appeared to be a communist takeover of the Congo".[15] Also considered as "crazy", having a "particularly violent character",[16] and referred to as "Africa's Castro",[17] Devlin was instructed to use any means of removing Lumumba from power and to replace him with a national leader sympathetic to US needs in the region. Mobutu now identified as the go-between, in September 1960 he organised a coup d'état covertly supported by the CIA. From that time, the

Gerald Rudolph Ford Jr. (b.1913 – d.2006) was the 38th President of the United States. The 40th Vice-President of the US, serving under Nixon, Ford authorised the funding of Holden Roberto's FNLA. (ThoughtCo)

Congo was governed by a succession of members of the Binza Group with the exception of Moise Tshombé, the former Prime Minister of Katanga. Tshombé being nominated as Prime Minister of the then Democratic Republic of the Congo (DRC) in July 1964, the United States was in the midst of providing financial and military assistance to the Congolese government in order to defeat communist-backed rebellion. The problem for the United States being that Tshombé was seen as an agent for a possible French-led takeover of the Congo, the US again chose to support Mobutu in a second coup d'état that took place in September 1965. Ousting Tshombé, the US continued to underpin Mobutu's regime with more financial and military assistance. It supplied the men and equipment that would be used in the formation of a naval force needed to protect the Congo's maritime border with Tanzania,[18] and when France and Belgium backed mercenary operations intended to depose Mobutu in 1966 and 1967. US relations with Mobutu also explain why the US chose to support Holden Roberto in the Angolan War of Independence. In addition to Roberto being Mobutu's brother-in-law, albeit through tenuous links,[19] in early 1963 the MPLA recruited between 3,500 and 7,000 Katangese Gendarmes exiled in Angola after the defeat of Tshombé's forces.[20] The MPLA seizing the Gendarmes' hatred of Mobutu, it was to use them in the fight against the FNLA.

If Mobutu managed to retain his grip over a country that became Zaire in 1971, it was partly due to significant increases in the price of copper between 1967 and 1970 that saw the Congolese economy grow by around 10 percent per year.[21] Though this grip was coupled by US suspicions that Mobutu was squandering the Congo's wealth and that most of its people remained affected by deep poverty,[22] the US maintained support for Mobutu due to developments taking place in Angola. Despite growing doubts surrounding Mobutu's leadership, US loyalty to the Congolese leader was based on his opposition to the MPLA. Mobutu illustrated this opposition at a meeting that took place either in Kinshasa or in Washington itself. On 4 August 1970, for example,[23] he used the ogre of the communist threat presented by the MPLA and the Soviet Union to persuade US officials to provide more support for the FNLA.[24] Ensuring Nixon's support for his own political and economic survival over the next four years – US companies such as Reynolds continuing to invest hundreds of millions of dollars in the Congo[25] – Mobutu's relations with Roberto were equally important to Gerald Ford. At a meeting held in Washington shortly after Nixon had resigned, Kissinger was eager to impress on a Zairian delegation that in spite of the recent

US anti-war activist groups such as the "US Out of Angola Committee" were virulent opponents of Nixon and Ford's foreign policies likening the intervention in Angola to war in Vietnam. (US Out of Angola Committee)

Seymour Hersh (b.1937), an American investigative journalist and political author. In 1969, Hersh exposed the My Lai Massacre and in 1974 reported on alleged abuses carried out by the United States Intelligence Community. (USIC)

changes US policy towards Zaire had not changed. Kissinger stating that "our relations with Zaire are of very great importance to the United States" and that Zaire was one of the key countries in the world and a king-pin in our policies toward Africa",[26] he was asked that in view of Portugal's decision to withdraw from Angola, the US should consider backing Holden. Kissinger's response being that Mobutu's views were always taken into "serious account",[27] he also gave the assurance that Mobutu was always welcome in the United States and that Ford attached "very great importance" to the relations between the two countries.[28] The conclusion of the meetings between Kissinger and Zairian delegates including Foreign Minister Umba di Lutete was that the CIA planned to "increase substantially" its payments to Roberto.[29] An amount which remains undisclosed, the payments were made to assure Mobutu that the US was "sympathetic" to his concerns about the future regime of an independent Angola, CIA Director William

Frank Church (right: 1924 – d.1984) was a Democrat Party Senator from Idaho. A protégé of President Lyndon B. Johnson, Church headed the so-called Church Committee created in 1975 to investigate alleged abuses carried out by the USIC. This photograph shows him with the future CIA Director and US President George Bush Snr.

Colby informed Kissinger that the payments were designed to help Mobutu during a "critical time in his career".[30]

A further payment to Roberto being approved by the 40 Committee in January 1975[31] – an amount ensuring that Angola did not become a communist nation[32] – in May 1975 Ford directed that a study of United States policy towards Angola be drawn up by the NSC's Inter-departmental Group for Africa (IGA), and that it should be forwarded and reviewed by 30 June in order to be presented to Ford.[33] The directive in question entitled National Security Study Memorandum (NSSM) 224, its goal was to provide a full evaluation of the situation in Angola. Focusing on aspects such as the potential in Angola for civil strife, the relative political, economic and military strengths of the three independence movements, and the role of Portugal, South Africa, the USSR and China in Angola, significantly Kissinger requested that the report also evaluate the likely Congressional and public attitudes towards "alternative" United States policies.[34] An obvious reference to the possibility of the US intervening overtly and militarily in Angola, Kissinger's remark was also a reference to a number of issues that affected the Ford administration's decision-making powers at the time. Effectively, whereas Ford saw involvement in Angola as a means of reversing what was perceived by some observers as "deteriorating prestige and credibility" on the international stage and provided him with the opportunity to demonstrate that he would not hesitate to use force against communist-backed aggression,[35] the United States had only very recently withdrawn from the Vietnam War. The American public and the US Congress very likely to oppose intervention in another foreign conflict, matters had been made worse for Ford since December 1974 with the publication in the New York Times of an article detailing CIA operations over the years.[36] Written by investigative journalist, Seymour Hersh, the article described a series of attempts by the CIA to assassinate foreign leaders. Dubbed the "Family Jewels", in response to Hersh's accusations, on 27 January 1975, the US Senate set up a Select Committee to investigate the claims. Known officially as the United States Senate Committee to Study Governmental Operations with Respect to Intelligence Activities, but known informally as the Church Committee,[37] as we shall see, the setting up of this commission was to severely restrict the scope of CIA activities in regards to Angola. The context therefore seeming to rule out any overt involvement, Ford was nevertheless left with no alternative but to keep faith with the CIA and to entrust them with covert operations in Angola. The name given to the operation was IA/FEATURE.

Operation IA/FEATURE: Planning

The IGA's report not due for submission until 30 June 1975, in the meantime, a series of further meetings took place in the White House and at CIA HQ in Langley to discuss the overall dynamics of the operation that was about to take place. The first was a meeting of the 40 Committee which gathered on 5 June and whose attendees included Kissinger, William P. Clements, Joseph J. Sisco, William Colby, Lt. General Brent Sowcroft and Lt. General John Pauly. The three main components of covert operations being represented then, the discussion turned towards how weapons could be transferred to the FNLA. The reply coming from William G. Hyland (Deputy National Security Advisor) that arms could be supplied using Mobutu, another question raised was whether the US should be supporting Roberto at all given that the FNLA leader spent so little time in Angola. This pointing to the fact that Roberto had little support outside northern Angola, Colby wondered whether support should not be provided instead to Jonas Savimbi of the UNITA.[38] Though Kissinger and Sisco feared that giving money to "everybody" risked diluting the impact of any operation (Kissinger pointing out that the CIA had used so-called "spray tactics" in Chile but still had lost to the communists),[39] a CIA Intelligence Information Cable dated 9 June told of Mobutu and Savimbi had met privately in Kinshasa on 28 May. Mobutu raised his concerns that Roberto was not being given the full picture by his field commanders in Angola. Stating that Savimbi's version of events was a more faithful representation, another issue – as raised in Washington – was Roberto's refusal to enter Angola. Mobutu stating that this was due to Roberto's fear of assassination should he return, but Savimbi replying that he would be seen as a coward if he did not, Mobutu's answer was that he had since terminated his assistance to Roberto and was likely to favour Savimbi's initiatives in the future.[40] Whether or not there had been a breach between Mobutu and Roberto, as Savimbi suspected, in Washington the preliminary plans to covertly support a "major effort to prevent a Neto takeover in Angola" were under way.[41]

It was believed that any US covert action in Angola should fall under three categories. Firstly, inasmuch as financial aid, this would be equal to the amounts received by the MPLA; secondly, political action should be taken to avoid civil war in Angola and to promote a Roberto-Savimbi coalition; and, thirdly, proposed covert military action consisted of supplying arms to Mobutu so that he could resupply the FNLA and possibly UNITA from his own stocks. To reassure Mobutu, the plan was to reassure him that the United States would "make good his losses".[42] The author of the report believing that the MPLA's best chance to dominate Angola was to push the FNLA back into the Bakongo tribal area, then crush UNITA militarily, it was envisaged that external actors such as Kenya's Kenneth Kaunda or the OAU could be used to either provide political advice to Savimbi, or to send a peacekeeping force to Angola. Another option being to encourage the "fragmentation of the MPLA" by "breaking off" some of Neto's lieutenants, a third option was to "inspire greater attention in the world press to the staging of arms from the USSR through Brazzaville and other issues".[43] While this report provides us with an insight into the political mechanics used in CIA covert operations, at the same time it provides valuable information on how operations were organised from a military point of view. In telling us that the CIA had already envisaged that there would be an escalation in the fighting in Angola, interestingly we see that the CIA was once preparing to tread along well-worn paths used in a number of previous covert operations. This included using "weapons of both US and foreign origin" being "at hand in current stocks; we find that "communications gear and transport can be readily found".[44] The idea of hiring mercenaries interestingly rejected at this point due to the CIA not having the "umbrella of a legitimate government asking for help",[45] despite fears that the delivery by air of armaments would quickly be detected and would damage the political prospects of the FNLA and UNITA, some way had to be found of continuing the war as to stop it, the CIA believed, remained very much to the advantage of the MPLA. The conclusion, therefore, was that military aid should be extended to Mobutu with or without the aid of American or American-hired technical advisors. If the IGA's response to NSSM 224 produced on 13 June contradicted the CIA's findings in stating that Ford should actively promote a peaceful settlement,[46] once again Mobutu's influence over US decision-making in regards to Central and Southern Africa tipped the balance in favour of active US military participation in Angola. Comparing the situation to US intervention in the Congo in the early 1960s and wondering why the US was not doing more in a country under greater communist threat, Mobutu, Kissinger believed, had concluded that the US had "written off the area". If so, the US had also abandoned

One of the rare occasions on which Holden Roberto ventured into Angola. Here he is pictured at Shannon's Forward Command Post.

FNLA HQ in Luanda. The MPLA forced the FNLA to leave the Angolan capital in July 1975.

Chinese military advisors to the FNLA were a frequent sight in Zaire.

him.[47] Although Kissinger estimation of Mobutu was extremely low, and at one point refereed to the Zairian leader as a "semi-savage" interested only in money,[48] he nevertheless accepted that given what had happened in Vietnam since US withdrawal that he had a point. Consequently, Kissinger requested that Mobutu's trusted friend Larry Devlin be sent to evaluate his thoughts on the Angolan situation before definitive plans were submitted to Ford for approval.[49] With Cyrus Vance also discussing the evolution of events in Angola sometime before his return to Washington on 27 June, he reported to Kissinger that Mobutu had suggested the US give "substantially more money to Holden and Savimbi". This being because Holden's superiority had disappeared due to Soviet shipments of weapons to the MPLA, Vance's belief was that payments amounting to several millions should be made and that the CIA should act as quickly as possible if the MPLA were to be stopped from establishing power in Luanda on 11 November.

The meeting on 27 June also involving Walter Cutler, the CIA's Country Director for Zaire, and Edward Mulcahy, the Acting Assistant to Secretary of State, Nathaniel Davis, discussions quickly turned towards the broader shape of what was now an inevitable US intervention. Vance evoked the point that the US had an advantage over the MPLA through its having a "continuous territory" through which weapons could be supplied (Kaunda having stopped MPLA weapons being transported across Zambia), and both Cutler and Mulcahy agreed that the CIA could be purchase arms in Europe and shipped to Angola. The agency possessing warehouses in Europe, further transportation could be provided through the CIA's stock of C-130s. Once weapons such as M-16s and bazookas had arrived in Zaire, they would be transported across the border by truck.[50]

At a meeting of the NSC held during the afternoon of 27 June, CIA Director William Colby raised the spectre of the US not being able to supply funds large enough to "wrap it up quickly" and, with the CIA's "current exposure" to "get away without a great deal of criticism".[51] Colby's comments in reference to the Church Committee's investigation into CIA activities and a good degree of negative public opinion having been generated since December 1974, Ford emerged as the strongest advocates of ignoring "leakage and scandal" in the present situation. For Ford, what counted was that if "you were going to do something, you're going to have to do it in a meaningful fashion". "Doing nothing" being unacceptable in Ford's view, it would appear that his position was based on the contents of an attachment provided to the meeting's attendees. The main points of this attachment were that the situation in Angola was highly unstable; new fighting could erupt at any time; the oil-rich enclave of Cabinda was a tinderbox; outside powers

Weapons for the FNLA were flown by the USAF to Kinshasa before being transported to Ambriz in northern Angola. Aircraft chartered from Air Zaire – and its subsidiary, Zaire Aero Service, a Vickers Viscount of which is visible in this photograph – have played an important role in this transportation.

As for UNITA, it was supplied with weapons delivered by the Zambian Air Force (ZAF), a C-47 of which can be seen in this photograph. British-made Land Rovers were also at UNITA's disposal.

supplying weapons remained a key factor; Roberto had had little success in finding assistance; and Mobutu was experiencing severe problems in regards to Zaire's domestic situation. Moreover, and echoing what influenced Nixon's choosing of the 'Tar Baby' option in 1969, considerations on the reaction Rhodesia and South Africa to an MPLA victory were essential to understanding what finally convinced Ford to approve IA/FEATURE. Effectively, the attachment underlined that continued fighting in Angola would exacerbate the confrontation between black and white Africa. The attachment stated that South Africa was particularly concerned that a communist regime might support guerrilla activity in Namibia; a "hostile or unstable Angola" would increase South African pressure on the US to support its domestic and international policies.[52] Concluding with the remark that this would complicate US efforts to promote peaceful solutions to Southern Africa's racial problems, South Africa was not believed to be planning any action to counter threats at that time.[53] As shown in a previous section, this proved to be an erroneous appraisal.

During the first two weeks of July, the Angolan programme began to get off the ground through a meeting of the 40 Committee on Monday 14 July. The members of this group whose mission it was to oversee covert operations still with doubts over how much money should be given and to who,[54] at the end of the meeting it was requested that the CIA finalise its plan for covert action and that it submit its report as early as possible. Drafted by the CIA's Africa Division, the paper entitled "Plan for Covert Action – Angola" was submitted to the Committee just two days later on 16 July.[55] Approved the same day by Ford according to the memoires of John Stockwell, the Angolan programme leader, on 17 July Kissinger expressed his wish to provide a $20 million aid package to Zaire in what he referred to as the "Mobutu plan".[56] No sooner had this payment been made to Mobutu, on 24 July the State department received a telegram from the US Embassy in Zaire to report on Cyrus Vance's meeting with Mobutu that had taken place the day before. Mobutu was particularly concerned with what type of weapon needed to be supplied and put the emphasis on receiving 5,000 M-16 rifles and one to two months ammunition as quickly as possible. His second priority being to receive anti-tank weaponry to replace what he had already transferred to the FNLA, Mobutu impressed on Vance the need for urgent action given that "The Soviets are continuing to send arms into Angola while we are sitting here talking". Following what was a familiar outburst from the Zairian leader, the embassy's recommendation was that Washington make its final review and costing of the plan.[57] The urgency contained in the embassy telegram leading to Kissinger convening yet another meeting on 25 July, Kissinger decided that the M-16s would be taken from the CIA's stocks and demanded that William Colby organise their shipment to Zaire.[58] Colby then being informed on 28 July that a "higher authority" had approved the plan for covert action,[59] on Tuesday 29 July the first planeload of arms left South Carolina for Kinshasa.[60] This cargo was quickly followed by a shipment of arms carried aboard the SS *American Champion*, a type C4-S 57 cargo ship.

The Angola Programme in Action

Shortly before the first cargo of US-supplied weapons left for Kinshasa John Stockwell arrived in Washington fresh from service in Saigon. A 38-year-old field officer holding a GS-14 grade (Lieutenant Colonel), Stockwell had previously served as chief of the CIA's Lubumbashi base in Zaire, chief of station in Bujumbura in Burundi and chief of the CIA's Kenya-Uganda section. The CIA first became interested in recruiting Stockwell in 1963 after learning that he had spent part of his youth in the then Democratic Republic of the Congo. Speaking the local Tshiluba dialect fluently, Stockwell joined the CIA's training programme and became a full-time member of its staff in 1964.[61]

On arriving at the CIA's HQ in Langley on 30 July 1975, Stockwell made his way to the office of George Costello, the Africa chief of operations and deputy to Jim Potts, the Africa chief of division. Stockwell was informed of the recent weapons transfer, how much funding had been made available and that he was being made chief of the Angola Task Force. During a second meeting Stockwell learnt more about the weapons transfers that had already taken place and others that were due for the 3 August. The weapons in question were initially sourced from the CIA's warehouse in San Antonio, Texas; they were then transported by C-130 to Charleston, South Carolina from where United States Air Force (USAF) charged the CIA $80,000 to haul them across the Atlantic to Kinshasa in their cargo planes. As noted above, a further shipment was transported by the SS *American Champion* (at a cost of $500,000) and as noted by aviation historian, Victor Flintham, there were reports that some arms were taken to Negage (Uíge province of Angola) from US bases in Germany aboard C-54s or C-118s.[62]

John Stockwell, the head of the CIA's Operation IA/FEATURE. (adapted from photo published in *The Village Voice*).

Arms and Materiel delivered to Zaire for Angola programme

1. Armoured Vehicles

M-113 Armoured Personnel Carrier (APC)	12

2. Missiles

SA-7 'Grail' anti-aircraft (SAM)	50

3. Heavy weapons

106 mm recoilless rifles	14
4.2 in. mortars	38
60 mm, 81 mm, 82 mm mortars	1,272
3.5 in. rocket launchers	180
.50 cal, 12.7 mm heavy machine guns	64
RPG-7 grenade launchers	25

4. Machine guns, etc.

LAWs	9,413
M-79 40 mm grenade launchers	641
5.56 mm, 7.62 mm rifles	17,258
.30 cal. carbines	28,800
.45, 9 mm. SMGs	6,121
.45, 9 mm. pistols	1,668
Hand grenades	96,300

5. Vehicles

1/4-ton, 11/4-ton, 21/2-ton trucks	60
Trailers 11/2-ton	20
Swift boats 50 and 58 ft.	2
Rubber boats with motors	25

6. Ammunition

HEAT and HEP 106 mm.	3,140
HE mortar 120 mm.	1,000
HE, SP, and ILLUM mortar 4.2 in.	4,454
3.5 in. rounds for rocket launcher	1,980
HE, WP and ILLUM mortar rounds 81 mm.	16,799
HE, WP and ILLUM mortar rounds 60 mm.	64,620
M-79 40 mm. rounds	261,840
.50 cal. spot 106 mm. rounds	17,200
.50 cal., 12.7 mm.	112,726
.30 cal., 7.62 x 54 mm.	2,811,947
7.62 mm., 5.56 mm rifle rounds	14,255,866
.30 cal. carbine rounds	5,332,386
7.62 x 39 mm.(AK-47)	290,400
.45 cal., 9 mm SMG rounds	3,508,807

7. Miscellaneous

PRC-10, PRC-25, PRC-77 radios	641
ANGRC-9/87 radios	100
AN/WRC-46/47 radios	12
FM-1B, FM-5B radios	68
TRA-921 radio	108
RF-301 radio	25
HT-2A radio	50
TAR-224 radio	6
BEL-990 radio	4

Tents, medical supplies, fieldgear, vehicle parts, boat parts, aircraft parts, demolition materials, combat rations

Adapted from Stockwell, pp.283-284

Weapons transported by the *American Champion* arriving in Matadi between 3-9 August 1975

1. Rifles and Anti-Tank

M-16s	9,000
Ammunition M-16	5 million rounds
M-72 Light Anti- Tank Weapons (LAWS)	6,000

2. Other equipment

Swift boats (57ft. and 55 ft.)	2
.50 calibre machine guns with tripod (probably M-6)	50
81mm mortar (probably M252)	53
4.2 inch mortar (probably M2)	18
PRC-77 Portable Transceiver	300
BA4386 Batteries	3,000

3. Ammunition

.50 calibre machine gun	102,000 rounds
81 mm high explosive (HE) mortar	9,360 rounds
smoke grenades (probably M18)	1,080

4. Vehicles

Ford M151-A1 1/4-ton 4x4 utility truck	20
Kaiser M-715 11/4-ton utility truck	20
M35-A2 21/2-ton 6x6 utility truck	20
M-105 11/2-ton utility truck	20
Other large trucks	60
Trailers	20

5. Tents and Material

GP Medium tents	500
Puncture-resistant boots	10,000
Socks	20,000
Webbing	5,000 belts

6. Extra equipment referred to by Stockwell as "30. cal Package Plus Ecess"(sic)

Carbines (28,800); .45 calibre pistols (1,350); .45 calibre sub-machine guns (5,379); .30 calibre LMG (1,814); 3.5 in. rocket-launchers (380); 60 mm mortars (999); ANPRC-10 radio (97); ANGRC 9/87 radios (90); 7.3 million rounds of ammunition.

7. Equipment referred to by Stockwell as "7.62 Cal. Package)

Rifles (5,810); 9 mm cal. pistols (350); 9 mm cal. SMGs (810); 7.62 cal. LMGs (460); 40 mm grenade-launchers (620); 66 mm rocket-launchers (1,800); 60 mm mortars (140); ANPRC 25/77 radios (270); Racal TRA92 radios (70); 8.2 million rounds of ammunition.

8. Miscellaneous

60 trucks
20 trailers
25 rubber boats with motors

Adapted from: Stockwell, *In Search of Enemies*, p.279

Between 3-9 August IA/FEATURE entered into full swing: the CIA's Office of Logistics were coordinating weapons transfers with help from the Special Operations Group (SOG),[63] the CIA in Washington was coordinating with the CIA in Liberia to arrange for the refuelling of planes at Monrovia, and arrangements had been made with the CIA's station in Kinshasa to make sure that Zairian trucks were at Ndjili airport ready to offload weapons and transfer them onto trucks heading for Angola. With Kenneth Kaunda also having agreed to send weapons to Savimbi,[64] it was time for Stockwell to go to Zaire and Angola to get first-hand experience of how and if the added weight of US aid was changing the context of the war.

If Stockwell's visit to Angola from 20 August 1975 revealed that Roberto had been convinced to return to Angola and that UNITA appeared to be far better prepared for war than the FNLA, his return to

Independence Day in Angola. 11 November 1975 marked the end of nearly 500 years of Portuguese colonialism in Africa.

A pair of BRDM-2s of 9 BRIM – the FAPLA's first mechanised infantry brigade – rolling down the streets of Luanda during a parade in celebration of independence, on 11 November 1975.

An MPLA fighter celebrates the end of Portuguese rule.

Washington five days later showed that the United States had become fully committed to supporting both sides. USAF C-141s continued to transport weapons destined for Angola to Kinshasa throughout September and October, the SS *American Champion* had sailed from South Carolina with a cargo of more equipment at the end of August, and 83 CIA officers were dispatched to the Kinshasa, Luanda, Lusaka and Pretoria stations to manage the air, ground, maritime and propaganda branches of IA/FEATURE. Funding had also increased: in addition to money made available to the CIA on 18 July, on 20 August 1975 Ford authorised another \$10.7 million bringing the total so far to \$24.7 million.[65]

By early September, the arrival of foreign-made weapons and funding was having a profound effect on the internal dynamics of the Angolan conflict. The MPLA's Katyusha 122 mm rockets were producing devastating results and had pushed back the FNLA from Caxito in northern Angola; and not possessing the means to counter the advances of its adversaries the FNLA turned to Mobutu and South Africa for assistance. Feeling increasingly threatened, the Zairian leader had indeed begun to take matters into his own hands and on 11 September Mobutu dispatched his elite Fourth and Seventh Commando Battalions to Ambriz aboard C-130s and, for a while it appeared that the armed wing of the FNLA, the National Liberation Army of Angola (ELNA) was gaining the upper hand: Caxito was retaken by a combined force of Zairian, ELNA and Portuguese soldiers on 17 September beginning an advance on Luanda; a second Zairian force reinforced the Front for the Liberation of Cabinda (FLEC) in order to combat MPLA troops operating in the enclave. This invasion that took place in October 1975 was supported by the United States: it flew in a 1,000-man arms package aboard a Piper PA-23 Aztec, a Cessna 172, a Cessna 180, a Cessna 310, a Turbo Commander, an Alouette III, and a Mooney;[66] and CIA officers based in Kinshasa were used to coordinate operations.[67]

This, however, had little effect as by then the MPLA was being supported by Cuban forces, in the meantime UNITA had been struggling to overcome the MPLA in conflict being fought on two flanks. Effectively, Katanganese forces fighting for Neto held back Savimbi's forces at Luso (Luena) in the Moxico Province, and Cuban-backed MPLA halted the advance of UNITA troops just outside of Lobito. Then pressing home the advantage, the MPLA made its way inland towards Nova Lisboa (Huambo). Cutting off the city's water and electricity supplies, this was enough to persuade Savimbi to accept more assistance from South Africa. On 21 September, the South Africa group of advisors arrived at Savimbi's HQ at Silva Porto and began the training of UNITA troops. Savimbi had also come under enormous pressure from Zambia's Kenneth Kaunda who wanted the FAPLA controlled Benguela Railway to be open for 11 November.

As described in previously, while Mobutu's troops were attacking Caxito on 14 October 1975 Task Force Zulu crossed the Angolan border from Rundu in South West Africa to take a more active role in the Angolan conflict. Led by Colonel Koos van Heerden, Task Force Zulu made rapid progress through southern Angola reaching Pereira d'Eça on 14 October, Rocadas on 20 October, João de Almeida on 22 October, Sá da Bandeira on 24 October, and Moçâmedes on 27 October. By 2 November both Task Force Zulu and Foxbat had reached the outskirts of Catengue. This was followed by an advance on Benguela, which was taken on the 5 November, and further moves northward to take Lobito on 7 November. The South African-backed forces making rapid progress towards Luanda, meanwhile other combat units had moved through central Angola. The Katanganese had been driven out of Luso and moved to Texeira da Sousa. Three days before independence, on 8 November 1975 the Zairian/ELNA forces began their own advance on Luanda. Crossing the Quifangondo plain some 12 miles north of Luanda, they were supported by four BL 5.5-inch Medium Guns manned by South Africans and two 130mm long-barrel M-46 field guns that Mobutu reportedly obtained from North Korea.[68] Known also as the Battle of Death Road, the Battle of Quifangondo was the last

One of the last remaining Portuguese regular army soldiers to leave the Angolan capital. Visible in the rear is an AML-60 of the Portuguese Army.

The Portuguese government generally supported the MPLA and was present in Luanda on 11 November 1975 to ensure independence passed as peaceably as possible. This motorised column of Portuguese Army troops (mostly mounted on Unimog light trucks) was photographed while moving in direction of the port.

effort by the FNLA and South African forces to unseat the MPLA in Luanda and to claim the spot as the legitimate state power in an independent Angola.

If Roberto's forces had endeavoured to take control of the Quifangondo plains as early as August 1975, the attack launched on 10 November pitched them against well organised FAPLA forces backed by Cubans and a number of Stalin's Organs. Given the go-ahead by Roberto, a preliminary bombardment carried out by South African Canberras was accompanied by the SADF using three 140 mm howitzers to soften up the enemy. While this was taking place, a group of commandos led by Colonel Santos e Castro would capture the bridge over the Bengo River and the main attacking force comprising 2,000 FNLA and 1,200 Zairians would advance towards Luanda. Concurrently, this larger force was supported by 120 Portuguese mercenaries, 12 armoured cars and six jeep-mounted recoilless guns. As the armoured cars advanced they were hit by a barrage of fire from machine guns, mortar and artillery. Incapacitating four of the armoured cars and inflicting heavy casualties, the Cubans then fired two 20-rocket salvos from their BM-21s. Killing over 120 FNLA and disabling around a dozen vehicles, the attack quickly disintegrated.[69]

The defeat at Quifangondo was one from which the FNLA never really recovered even if the fighting was to continue for another four months. Even as the battle raged, the Portuguese High Commissioner was preparing to grant Angola independence, and as midnight struck in Luanda thousands poured on to the streets to celebrate the end of nearly 500 years of Portuguese rule. On 11 November 1975, Agostinho Neto addressed the crowds and declared the establishment of the People's Republic of Angola (PRA). The new state was immediately recognised by some 30 countries, the Soviet Union and Cuba amongst them, and in Ambriz the FNLA and UNITA declared the establishment of the Popular Democratic Republic of Angola (PDRA). Headquartered in the newly named Huambo, this was recognised by no other country. What was left for the MPLA and the Cubans to achieve now was the defeat of Task Force Zulu, a much greater threat than the FNLA and Mobutu's troops.

4
From Independence to the Luanda Trial of Mercenaries

Despite UN Secretary-General Kurt Waldheim calling for the three Angolan factions to lay down their arms and expressing support for OAU efforts to bring about a ceasefire on 13 November,[3] the London *Times* and the *Chicago Tribune* reported that Russian military personnel including fighter pilots, tank crews and advisors had joined Cuban troops in assisting the MPLA. 400 arrived on 14 November alone.[4] The strength of Cuban forces was believed to have risen from anywhere from 200 to 4,000, and was being added to by the arrival in Luanda on 17 November of 30-60 Cuban specialists in guerrilla warfare.[5] US estimates put the number of Cuban advisors at as many as 3,000.[6] To counter this 'threat', South African troops continued to operate deep into Angolan territory in support of both the FNLA and UNITA. Though the existence of any South African operations was denied by Foreign Minister Dr. Hilgard Muller, claims that UNITA had captured 20 Russians, 35 Cubans and 30 Mozambicans seemed to suggest – given its poor record so far – that the SADF was continuing to intervene.

The mood amongst the 40 Committee members that met on 14 November 1975 was one that was to be expected given the establishment of a communist inspired regime at the head of a newly independent nation no longer reliant on or influenced by a NATO-allied nation like Portugal. And, though, war continued to rage in Angola, the belief was that the MPLA would remain in power so long as it continued to be supplied with Cuban and Soviet weaponry.[7] The number of Cubans that had arrived in Angola was seen as being a "new factor" on the question of which side would dominate military proceedings in the coming months, but more particularly, there were concerns that MiG fighters would soon appear in the skies over Angola and provide a psychological blow that would finally defeat anti-MPLA forces. Though the 40 Committee was at that point unaware that 12 MiG-21s and 10 MiG-17s were about to be delivered to Luanda International and then assembled by Soviet technicians, for operations by Cuban pilots and ground personnel,[8] this did not stop the CIA's Jim Potts from evoking the possibility of sending FIM-43 Redeye or British-made Shorts Blowpipe: man-portable air defence systems (MANPADs) that had just entered service. Another option was using around 50 Soviet-made 9K32 Strela-2 (ASCC/NATO-code

Timeline of Mercenary Activities in Angola, 1975-1976

July 1975 – John Banks sets up the International Security Organisation (ISO) and recruits a mercenary force with the intention of invading Rhodesia.
August 1975 – Banks renames his company Security Advisory Services (SAS).
18 August 1975 – Lisbon newspaper *Diario de Noticias* reports that Portuguese mercenaries have arrived in Novo Lisboa (Huambo) from Rhodesia and have joined Roberto's forces.[1]
Late August 1975 – John Stockwell meets with a "Captain Bento" and Colonel Santos Castro, the commander of the Portuguese Liberation Army (ELP).
Late summer 1975 – France begins providing financial assistance to anti-MPLA forces to pay the salaries of mercenaries and regular troops as well as for the purchase of weapons. The $30 million is filtered through Mobutu.[2]
November 1975 – Costas Georgiou (aka "Colonel Callan") arrives in Angola.
10 November 1975 – Portuguese mercenaries take part in fighting at the Battle of Quifangondo.
21 November 1975 – The 40 Committee raises the question of using mercenaries to assist the FNLA and UNITA.
4 December 1975 – Ford Administration orders a further $25 million to be given to anti-MPLA forces.
12 December 1975 – It is reported that the Congress of Racial Equality (CORE) has recruited black US veterans to serve as medics in Angola.
13 December 1975 – It is reported that a number of US mercenaries have been recruited and are fighting MPLA forces in Angola.
23 December 1975 – South Africa takes the decision to gradually withdraw from Angola.
31 December 1975 – It is reported that attempts have been made to recruit Cuban exiles to fight with the FNLA.
10 January 1976 – The first of French mercenaries recruited by Bob Denard arrive in Kinshasa. They are given weapon training by CIA field officers.
12 January 1976 – Roberto aide Nick Hall arrives in London to recruit British mercenaries.
17 January 1976 – After meeting Hall, John Banks begins the recruitment of British mercenaries.
19 January 1976 – the first batch of British mercenaries arrive in Kinshasa.
20 January 1976 – British mercenaries arrive at the FNLA HQ in São Salvador.
Last week of January 1976 – Cuban/FAPLA forces advance northwards towards the border with Zaire.
30-31 January 1976 – the second batch of British mercenaries arrive at São Salvador.
2 February 1976 – Callan orders the Maquela Massacre.
First week of February 1976 – further armed confrontations with Cuban/FAPLA forces.
6 February 1976 – US mercenaries arrive in Angola.
7 February 1976 – American Gary Acker arrives in Angola.
14 February 1976 – a major confrontation with 2 Bon I of the FAPLA, led by Cubans, results in the deaths of a number of British mercenaries. Callan and several others are captured.
27 March 1976 – South Africa withdraws from Angola.
11-19 June 1976 – the Luanda Trial of mercenaries takes place.
10 July 1976 – Callan and three others are executed by firing squad.

'SA-7 Grail') sourced from Israel. Left on the table for another time and another meeting, theoretical discussions such as this were replaced by the more down-to-earth consideration of how to counter the Cuban forces that were moving up through Angola to Cabinda.[9] As observers in Luanda 'confirmed' the presence of Soviet-supplied MiGs on 26 November by asking themselves whether Cuban, Soviet or even Portuguese pilots would be used to fly them (actually, not one 'MiG' was in Angola by the time, and eventually, all of those that were delivered were flown by Cuban pilots, only),[10] the immediate solution for US officials was to provide more funding to the FNLA/UNITA, or to purchase two Douglas AC-47 Spooky gunships to assist them in their fight against the MPLA.

Operation IA/FEATURE: The Mercenary Option

Although Ford did authorise a further $25 million to be given to US-friendly Angolan forces via the CIA's contingency funds on or around 4 December as reported by the *New York Times*,[11] a more direct approach in preventing the Soviet Union from gaining a foothold in Angola was suggested firstly by South African Prime Minister P.W. Botha on 27 November,[12] and by Brent Sowcroft and General George Brown, the Chairman of the Joint Chiefs of Staff. Effectively, at a 40 Committee meeting that took place on 21 November both officials raised the question of whether the CIA should not be looking to hire mercenaries.[13] No doubt, Sowcroft and Brown recalled how the CIA had used mercenary forces on many previous occasions and that it had recruited Cuban exiles to form mercenary air and maritime forces in the Congo. Later, they would doubtless become aware of reports in the *Boston Sunday Globe* that "scores of American mercenaries" had been recruited by FNLA and UNITA agents in the United States were already fighting in Angola and that hundreds more were due to arrive.[14] Additionally, they would no doubt have learnt of further reports published in the *Washington Post* on 12 December

Colonel Gilberto Santos e Castro discusses tactics with Holden Roberto at the FNLA HQ in Ambriz in August 1975. (Author's collection)

Many of the mercenaries were loyal to ELNA forces or, like Santos Castro, were members of the Portuguese Liberation Army. (ELP)

Castro (centre) commanded around 120 White Angolans or Portuguese veterans loyal to the FNLA. (Author's collection)

1975 that the Congress of Racial Equality (CORE) was recruiting black American military veterans for service in Angola.[15] These reports gained credence just two days later when Roy Innis, the national director of CORE affirmed that he was recruiting "Afro-American troops" for "humanitarian aid and as "peacekeeping forces".[16] Later, in February 1976, in an interview with the New York Times, Innis confirmed that that 300 black veterans were to be sent to Angola in mid-March 1976 as combat medics and that 1,000 more were being screened by his organisation in New York, Washington and Baltimore. The salaries of these "medics" would be paid by UNITA.[17]

It remains unclear whether the "several American mercenaries" reportedly working as instructors for UNITA forces were among those recruited by CORE or if they belonged to a separate mercenary group. Supposedly based at a camp around 100 miles east of Huambo according to the *Washington Post*,[18] the presence of any US mercenaries in Angola denied by William Colby in a statement published by the *Washington Post* two days later.[19] However, the possibility that there was, indeed, another group, and that this group was sponsored by the CIA gained a degree of

Because of the immense distances and the lack of good roads, the CIA went to great lengths to provide its mercenaries in Angola with plentiful air support. Lack of financing prohibited it from purchasing the necessary aircraft outright. However, in the overall chaos left in the wake of Portuguese withdrawal, its operatives were able to find plenty of suitable replacements. Among them was at least one Cessna 180G or 180H of unknown origin and appearance: the main illustration here is an example found abandoned by advancing South African troops at Huambo airport. Alternatively, the aircraft in question might have carried the standard livery for 180s: top of the fuselage and streaks in dark red, applied atop either white (as shown inset) or highly-polished metal. As far as it is known, this aircraft was deployed for utility purposes only, and was never armed. (Artworks by Tom Cooper)

According to reports provided by Cuban pilots, the most-dangerous CIA-operated aircraft was a Beechcraft 99-B55 Baron. Indeed, while armed with a single 7.62mm Browning M1919 machine gun (installed in the centre window on the left side), this model is said to have engaged a FAPLA-operated Piper PA-32 Cherokee-6 in the Margrida Ranch area, in Sumbe, in early November. Then, it was reportedly used in an air strike on Luanda Radio Club on 8 November 1975. The only B55 Baron currently known to have been registered in either Angola or Zaire was this example, probably operated by Air Congo/Air Zaire since October 1964, before being sold to a private owner in Belgium around October 1974. Nothing is known about its whereabouts the following year but, considering the reach of the CIA's 'tentacles', it is perfectly possible that it saw a 'tour of duty' with the agency before being returned to its private owner in Belgium as OO-GGH. (Artwork by Tom Cooper)

One of at least two bi-motor light aircraft known to have been operated by the CIA's mercenaries over Angola in 1975-1976 was reported to have been this Cessna 310II. Apart from it being stolen from Ugandan dictator Idi Amin, no other details about its subsequent service or livery are known, other than what is shown here (including a white overall, and either light blue, or washed-out dark blue streak and tip of the fin) – which is actually its condition as when seen for the last time, abandoned at Kindu airport, in eastern Congo in late 1998. Either this Cessna, or one of the CIA-operated B55 Barons (or a Piper PA-32 Cherokee-6, or Piper A-44 Seminole…) was involved in the second air combat of this campaign. This took place on 7 February 1976 when the crew of a CIA-operated aircraft ('identified' as a 'Cessna' by the Cubans) engaged a Cuban-operated Alouette III underway over the M'banza-Congo area by firing small-arms from its windows. The clash ended inconclusively. (Artwork by Tom Cooper)

For hauling the necessary ammunition, armament, equipment, and supplies from the USA to Zaire, and then from different air bases in Zaire closer to the frontline, the CIA chartered several Lockheed C-130E/Hs of the US Air Force and the Zairian Air Force respectively. As of 1975, all of these bore the same camouflage pattern: dark tan (FS30219), dark green (FS34079), and light green (FS34102) on top surfaces and sides, and light grey (FS36622) on the undersides. USAF aircraft bore their service titles and serials in white on the fin, and the unit insignia on the fuselage sides (inset is shown the C-130E 63-7778 from 463 Transport Air Wing), while the Zairian Hercules (main illustration) bore service titles in white on the forward fuselage, and their civilian-style registrations on the fin (9T-TCA was the first C-130H delivered to Zaire). (Artwork by Tom Cooper)

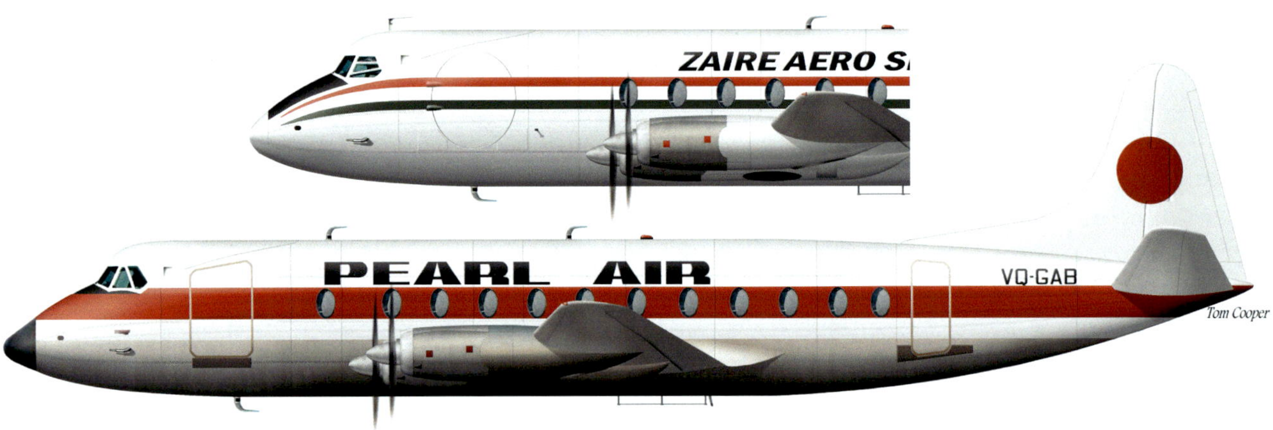

For operations between airfields in Zaire, and those closer to the combat zone, the CIA hired several civilian cargo aircraft. Foremost among these was the gaudily-marked Vickers Viscount Type 806 of the civilian air freighter Pearl Air, from Grenada, registered as VQ-GAB, shown in the main illustration. Shown inset is the front portion of the Viscount Type 700s of the Zaire Aero Service (ZAS), an air freight subsidiary of Air Zaire that was officially established only in 1976. Both aircraft are reported to have flown several dozen supply flights into northern Angola. As far as it is known, neither ever came under the fire of the MPLA/FAPLA or its Cuban allies. (Artworks by Tom Cooper)

After the Belgian airline Sabena, the Zaire Aero Service was the second operator of the world's first and only 'swingtail' Douglas DC-4 Skymaster: essentially a C-54 (c/n 10452, originally manufactured for the US Army Air Force as C-54B serial number 42-72347), modified as an air freighter, the whole rear fuselage (with fin) of which could be opened to the right side to enable loading and unloading of oversized freight. As was usual for ZAS aircraft, most of its fuselage was painted in white with cheat lines in dark red and dark green. The rest of the airframe and wing were left mainly in bare metal. This aircraft survived adventures in Angola and was sold to Kinar Cargo in 1984 as 9Q-CBK: it crashed on M'bamou Island on the Congo River on 23 August 1988. (Artwork by Tom Cooper)

Despite intensive operations by CIA-chartered transports, and although the Cuban and Angolan armed forces have claimed that several aircraft were destroyed on the ground during their advance into northern Angola, only one aircraft has been confirmed as a kill: the Air Zaire-operated Fokker F.27-600 registered as 9Q-CLO. While on the ground at Lumbala airport, it was hit by at least one 240mm S-24 unguided rocket fired by MiG-21MFs piloted by Rafael del Pino and Benigno González Cortes on 13 March 1976, and burned out. Zairian dictator Mobutu charged the CIA US$300,000 as compensation for its loss. (Artwork by Luca Canossa)

While there are reports that CIA-recruited mercenaries operated several Aérospatiale SE.315B Alouette II and SE.316B Alouette III helicopters, the only example that could be positively identified was this Alouette III commandeered from the stocks of the Zairian Air Force. Painted in dark green overall, it bore a full service title on the boom, and the registration 9T-HT9 in white on the lower sides of the fuselage. Eventually, this helicopter was returned to Zaire. (Artwork by Tom Cooper)

South Africa acquired a total of 12 Lockheed C-130Bs during the mid-1960s. A decade later, they were still operated by No. 28 Squadron, SAAF, and were repainted in local versions of dark brown (BS381C/450) and olive drab (BS381C/298) applied following the standardised camouflage pattern on upper surfaces, the sides of the fuselage, and the undersides of the wing, while the undersides of the fuselage were in PRU-blue. All markings were reduced to the 'castle' roundels (also applied on undersides of the wing) and the serial in black on the rear fuselage. (Artwork by Tom Cooper)

Set up in November 1975 and operating well into 1976, the Soviet air-bridge to Luanda employed some of the largest transport aircraft in service at the time (the Antonov An-22, for example) but was primarily maintained by smaller aircraft. The Antonov An-12 being the main provider of this air-bridge for principally military purposes: many reached Angola bearing the markings of the Soviet national airline Aeroflot, even if operated by the Military Transport Aviation (*Voyenno-transportnoy aviatsii*, VTA) and equipped with a defensive tail-gun turret. Manufactured in 1963, the example illustrated here (registered as CCCP-11986) was one of the earliest An-12Bs and bore the full Aeroflot livery of white on the top and the sides of the fuselage. Other examples seen at Luanda International during this period were left in medium grey overall. (Artwork by Tom Cooper)

The first combat aircraft acquired by the FAPLA were 10 MiG-17Fs delivered from the USSR in late December 1975. All were painted in a bluish version of the light admiralty grey (BS381C/697) overall and received national markings in the form of Angolan national colours on the lower portion of the rudder, and roundels applied on top and bottom wing surfaces. Prefixed by 'C' (for *caça*, 'fighter'), their serials were C20 to C29. While simple to maintain and fly, the MiG-17F was poorly suited for fighter-bomber purposes. It could carry drop tanks *or* bombs weighing up to 125kg, *or* UB-16-57 pods (illustrated here) on its main underwing stations. However, it could not be equipped with any combination of drop tanks *and* armament. Combined with the 'hot and high' climate and terrain of Angola, this limited its combat range to just 125km. (Artwork by Tom Cooper)

In January 1976, Moscow delivered 12 MiG-21MFs to Luanda. Similarly to the MiG-17Fs, all were only operated by Cubans; however they were kept in reserve by Castro's standing order prohibiting combat deployments away from Luanda (withdrawn only in early February 1976). All the MiG-21MFs bore the standardised 'horns' camouflage pattern consisting of beige (BS381C/388) and olive drab (BS381C/298) on top surfaces and sides, with light admiralty grey (BS381C/697) on undersurfaces. National markings were applied in a similar fashion as on the MiG-17Fs with roundels at least on wing-undersurfaces (top inset). Known serials ranged from C41 to C53. The type's principal armament consisted of UB-16-57 pods for unguided rockets (left inset) and FAB-250M-62 general purpose bombs (shown on the inboard underwing pylon). To stretch their range, they could be equipped with 800-litre (shown on centreline) and 400-litre drop tanks (right inset). (Artwork by Tom Cooper)

In addition to a few privately owned cars, the Land Rover 2 was the primary utility vehicle of CIA and British-recruited mercenaries in Angola in 1975-1976. Most were civilian vehicles left behind by the Portuguese, or 'acquired by different means', and left in their original green or blue overall colour (left). Few were painted in camouflage patterns, and those that did usually bore splotches of brown, dark brown and two greens. Several were armed and deployed as 'technicals', usually with a single 12.7mm DShK 1938 heavy machine gun of Soviet design (right) but most likely of North Korean origin, and drawn from the stocks of the Zairian Army. (Artwork by David Bocquelet)

The Unimog was a range of multi-purpose all-wheel drive trucks designed by Daimler-Benz in the late 1940s. Tens of thousands were sold to different armed forces around the world, including those of Portugal, Congo/Zaire, France, South Africa and Rhodesia. Unsurprisingly, dozens were pressed into service by the CIA-recruited mercenaries assigned to the FNLA/ELNA. Most served as 'weapon carriers', or 'technicals' in modern-day jargon, with some retaining at least the lower part of the driver's cab. Others had this part completely removed. Several are known to have carried either a DShK or ZPU-1 heavy machine gun (left), while at least two – apparently drawn from former Portuguese stocks – were armed with 106mm M40 recoilless gun of US origin. (Artwork by David Bocquelet)

Besides a large number of Land Rover 2s, the mercenaries assigned to support the ELNA operated several Dodge WC-51 'Beeps'. These were vehicles from a prolific range of light, 4WD utility trucks manufactured en masse in the USA during the Second World War. Left behind by the Belgian Army, some of these were subsequently used by the Congolese/Zairians before being taken over by the CIA. As far as it is known, all were left in the US Army's Forest Green colour, applied overall. The mercenaries added armour plating to protect the front of the engine and used pedestal-mounted 7.62mm MG-3 machine guns of German origin (protected by a shield) placed on the flat bed in the rear. (Artwork by David Bocquelet)

The ELNA was bolstered by significant number of Panhard M3 armoured personnel carriers (left), in addition to AML-60 and AML-90 (right) armoured cars. Two AML-60s, one AML-90, and three M3s were obtained when a group of veteran Portuguese troops joined in July 1975, and 15 AMLs and M3s were provided by two FAZ battalions in October of the same year. While the majority of them were left in French Army dark green overall, some photographs indicate that several received makeshift camouflage in the form of splotches of brown and black. 'ELNA' was painted in white on the front and side panels. Most of ELNA's armour was destroyed during failed advances on Luanda and into the Cabinda Enclave in October-November 1975. Two mercenary-operated AML-90s were knocked out during the fighting for Cateco Cangola in mid-December 1975 while the last three were found abandoned in Tombôco on 8 February 1976. (Artwork by David Bocquelet)

The principal unit of the combined MMCA/FAPLA Northern Front offensive during the November 1975-February 1976 period (the time during which the FNLA/ELNA and CIA's mercenary forces in northern Angola were destroyed) was the 450-strong 2 Battalón de Infanteria (2 Bon I). The unit included a battery of 82mm mortars, and a platoon each of 75mm recoilless guns and heavy machine guns. For its advance, it was reinforced not only by the 1 Bon I, then 3 Bon I and 4 Bon I, but also by a battery of ZiS-3 guns, a battery of 82mm mortars, one platoon of ZPU-4 machine guns, a platoon of five Grad-1Ps, a contingent of 250 Cubans (including the 3 Bon IM of the FAR), and the crucial weapon of this campaign: a battery of BM-21 multiple rocket launchers, one of which is illustrated here. This had 40 122mm rocket tubes installed on the flat bed of a Ural-43201 truck. (Artwork by David Bocquelet)

The 3 Battalón de Infanteria (3 Bon I) – the third major Cuban-trained unit of the FAPLA – became operational shortly after the 2 Bon I, the unit that played a crucial role in the Northern Front offensive of the MMCA and the FAPLA during December 1975-February 1976. After the 'elite' 9 BRIM, it became the second unit to be equipped with BTR-60PB armoured personnel carriers. Moreover, it was one of very few FAPLA units to apply any kind of camouflage and markings on its vehicles as of 1975-76, as shown here. Together with a company of Cuban-operated T-34/85 medium tanks, the 3 Bon I followed in the wake of the 2 Bon I and its BTRs saw much combat during the final showdown with Callan's 'Killer Group'. (Artwork by David Bocquelet)

This NCO or junior officer of the FAR is shown wearing the older Cuban army uniform, curiously similar to the US design from the end of the Second World War, and which in 1976 was replaced by one including the lizard camouflage pattern. His cotton t-shirt was completed by pants closely resembling those of the US Army's M1944 uniform, and a green beret without a badge. Atop of this, he wore a canvas belt that was a copy of the M1943 of the US Army, and a Soviet-made magazine pouch. His armament consisted of the Soviet-made Tokarev TT-30 pistol, and the AKM assault rifle. (Artwork by Anderson Subtil)

In 1974, the FNLA introduced olive green uniforms provided from the stocks of the Zairian Army. This Bakongo soldier is further shown wearing a British-made canvas belt, an old canteen and a bag, and armed with the Chinese-made copy of the RPG-2 rocket-propelled grenade launcher - one of the most important weapons of the insurgency. (Artwork by Anderson Subtil)

While the mass of the FAPLA troops had simple uniforms in olive green overall, this soldier is shown wearing the campaign uniform manufactured in East German 'rain drop' pattern and Cuban-made 'botas rusas' boots, with a green beret with MPLA 'pin' (showing a yellow star on horizontally divided red and black fields). He is armed with a Walther P38 pistol, almost certainly drawn from stocks of the Portuguese Army, and a machette (locally known as a 'Catana') - a symbolic weapon in the war against the Portuguese colonialism. (Artwork by Anderson Subtil)

The few photographs of 'Colonel Callan' to become available before his arrest show him wearing a uniform in olive green overall, with British Army boots. Atop of this, he added a nylon vest and holster for his 9x19mm Browning hi-power semi-automatic pistol, a canvas belt with British 1958 pattern magazine pouches, a US-made canteen, and the M3 trench knife. His primary fire-arm was the old-fashioned .30 M2 carbine. (Artwork by Anderson Subtil)

ANGOLA CIVIL WAR
1975-1976

(Map by Anderson Subtil)

The ELP had links to General Spínola and to the CIA. Indeed, it is known that CIA field officers were providing ELNA/ELP forces with logistical assistance.

Portuguese mercenaries on the road from Caxito to Quifangondo, November 1975.

credence just a day later on 13 December when the *Black Panther Party Newspaper* and the *Christian Science Monitor* both published a statement by a former US soldier and resident of Kerman, California who claimed to be a veteran of the Korean and Vietnam wars and who also claimed that the CIA had provided him with the funds to recruit between 100-300 mercenaries for UNITA. Signed up for six months and paid $800 per month or signed up for 12 months and paid $1,200 monthly, Bufkin stated that initial funding came from Africa and that the mercenaries in question had arrived in Angola via South Africa while others had arrived via Zaire.[20]

Though some doubt has been cast concerning the veracity of Bufkin's claims of links with the CIA, a Rhodesian intelligence officer once describing Bufkin as a "nut case",[21] and Bufkin's time in Angola disputed by other sources,[22] there does appear to be elements of truth in his claims that US mercenaries were sent firstly to South Africa and that he acted as a recruiting agent either for the CIA or for the Federal Bureau of Investigation (FBI). Firstly, Bufkin's claims echo statements made by Bill Potts on 14 November – that South Africa was being pushed to pull out its regular forces and use mercenaries[23] – and, secondly, further support comes through witness statements provided to the House Committee on Foreign Affairs that gathered in Washington between 17-30 September 1980.[24] In statements relating to a certain Gary Acker (a former US Marine known to have served in Angola as we shall see later), the House Committee heard that Acker had replied to an advertisement in *The Sacramento Bee* newspaper that read "Hiring for Civil War in West Africa". Subsequently meeting Bufkin in Fresno, California, it was on 7 February 1976 that Acker arrived in Zaire from where he travelled to São Salvador, Angola on 10 February. Four days later, he was taken prisoner by Cuban forces as part of the British mercenary groups fighting in northern Angola at the time.

Another rumour given coverage at the end of December 1975 was that Cuban exiles were being lined up to fight in Angola. Bearing similarities to CIA clandestine operations in the 1960s in the Congo, the *New York Times* reported that Jose Antonio Prat, a veteran of the Bay of Pigs was being used as a recruiting agent in Miami. After service in Angola, Prat claimed that the group would be used to overthrow Fidel Castro.[25] Working with another Cuban exile named Pedro Martinez Castro, in a second interview published, this time, in the *Washington Post* of 9 January 1976 Prat had purportedly already recruited 365 men and that they were ready to be airlifted to Angola.[26] Again, an episode that does not appear to have come to fruition, Prat had, indeed, been a member of Brigade 2506, the Cuban exile invasion force used in an attempt to overthrow Fidel Castro on 17 April 1961.

Whether Bufkin's and Prat's claims held any truth or not, by that point the 40 Committee would have also known that Portuguese mercenaries had been fighting alongside ELNA forces as John Stockwell had met a number of them at Ambriz during his visit to FNLA HQ in late August 1975. Here, Stockwell encountered a certain "Captain Bento" and Colonel Santos Castro and together they discussed how White Angolans and Portuguese veterans of the Angola and Mozambique campaigns had integrated Roberto's forces. As seen earlier, Portuguese mercenaries fought alongside South African forces at the Battle of Quifangondo and many were members of the Portuguese Liberation Army (ELP), a group connected to General Spínola. Others had been members of the PIDE.[27] According to Castro, he could raise an army of some 600 Portuguese army veterans whom, he claimed, were awaiting orders in South Africa and were ready to intervene should Kissinger want to supply air tickets, $1,000 per man plus weapons.[28] Castro's

Portuguese mercenaries head to Quifangondo accompanied by FNLA troops.

Portuguese mercenaries used a variety of modes of transport.

Members of the ELP often had to equip themselves with whatever uniforms and equipment was available. Despite their efforts, attempts to defeat the MPLA was fast becoming a lost cause.

claims appear plausible given that in November 1975, South Africa needed help to pay mercenaries and comments made by Jim Potts and Staff General George Brown noted at the aforementioned 40 Committee meeting. What is more, South Africa was looking to withdraw its troops and replace them with mercenaries. This was because South Africa was facing a perilous situation at the time: the African National Congress (ANC) was becoming increasingly restless and the anti-apartheid Inkatha Freedom Party (IFP) had just been created by Mangosuthu Buthelezi; the buffer states of Mozambique and Rhodesia had either become independent or were at war; an oil embargo imposed by Arab states was punishing South Africa's economy; and the SWAPO was increasing its activity in South West Africa. The South Africa National Security Council finally took the decision to withdraw from Angola on 23 December 1975.

As Stockwell notes "mercenaries seemed to be the answer" to the needs of the FNLA/UNITA given their difficulty in making any headway in military terms. The Zairian commando battalions "were only slightly better", than the FNLA forces they joined, and so the CIA scoured the world for allies who could provide qualified advisors to insert into the conflict or, better still, professional regular army units able to overcome the MPLA and deliver the country to Roberto and Savimbi.[29] According to Stockwell the CIA canvassed moderate friends such as Brazil, South Korea, Belgium, Great Britain, France and even Portugal. Indeed, the possibility of recruiting French mercenaries was raised by Deputy Secretary of State Robert Ingersoll at a meeting held on 19 November.[30] After all, the French government had just given $1.5 million in ammunition to support Roberto and Savimbi, were just about to give another $5 million worth. The French were also supplying Mirage's to Zaire thus showing that President Giscard D'Estaing was sympathetic to their aims of friendly Angolan leaders as well as Mobutu's. The CIA even considered using Cuban exiles as it had done in the Congo some 10 years earlier and at Watergate in 1972. Nonetheless, this was ruled out as the Cubans in question now had green cards and would fall under the 40 Committee's ban on using American citizens. South Vietnamese refugees in America were also excluded due to their wish to build new lives in the USA and their reticence to be involved in a CIA war in Africa. Moreover, these refugees also held green cards.[31]

With Great Britain refusing at this point to entertain the idea of supplying "military advisors", using French mercenaries appeared to make good sense given their experience of African colonial conflicts and the fact that French Secret Services, the SDECE had been advising Savimbi for some time. The same services working hand-in-hand with MI6 put the CIA in touch with Bob Denard.[32] A veteran of the Congo Crisis having sought refuge in Angola in 1963 after the fall of Katanga, Denard had enormous experience of Africa and Africa conflicts due to his participation in wars in Biafra, Benin and Gabon. Denard agreed to provide 20 French mercenaries who would be employed to give "advice" to UNITA. Employed on a short-term basis, Denard wanted $500,000 up front to pay mercenaries who became known as 'Robin Hoods' or the 'French Hoods'. This was in respect to Denard being

Portuguese mercenaries could be found fighting alongside UNITA forces. Many were veterans of Portugal's war in Mozambique.

Two Portuguese commandos bearing the insignia of the FNLA. Note that the soldier behind is wearing a t-shirt bearing the insignia of the Commandos, a special forces unit in the Portuguese Army.

Portuguese mercenaries were well-armed professional soldiers with many years of experience fighting in Africa's colonial wars.

French mercenaries were recruited by Bob Denard. Their main area of activity was in the enclave of Cabinda where they provided assistance to the FLEC.

Despite plans to recruit hundreds of Portuguese mercenaries in December 1975, relatively few Portuguese could be found in Angola after the country's independence. These two are pictured in northern Angola in January 1976.

encrypted UNROBIN/1 by the CIA and the programme itself UNHOOD.[33] The money was to be paid to Mobutu, then diverted to a bank in Luxembourg. The first 11 of Denard's mercenaries arrived in Kinshasa on 10 January 1976 and were given training on how to use SA-7 ground-to-air missiles by CIA weapons experts. They were then flown to Silva Porto in a plane chartered for Operation IA/FEATURE. The remaining French mercenaries arrived on 27 January. Stockwell notes that one of them was obviously a French agent.[34]Although D'Estaing had said that he would be able to provide a thousand French mercenaries for Angola only a short time before Denard's recruits arrived,[35] the intervention of such a small number of mercenaries operating solely in Cabinda and providing assistance limited to training was never going to be enough to push back the MPLA and as many as 9-12,000 regular Cuban troops.

Meanwhile, the CIA had pushed ahead with a simultaneous programme and had been carrying out negotiations with Santos Castro. A CIA officer met with Castro in Madrid in December 1975, and the plan was to recruit 300 mercenaries. Castro had already opened a bank account in Berne into which CIA payments were to be made, and Castro received $55,000 that was paid directly into the account with another $55,000 given in untraceable cash. Three hundred return plane tickets between Lisbon and Kinshasa were provided, and funds to cover medical expenses, salaries and bonuses also formed part of the agreement. The mercenaries

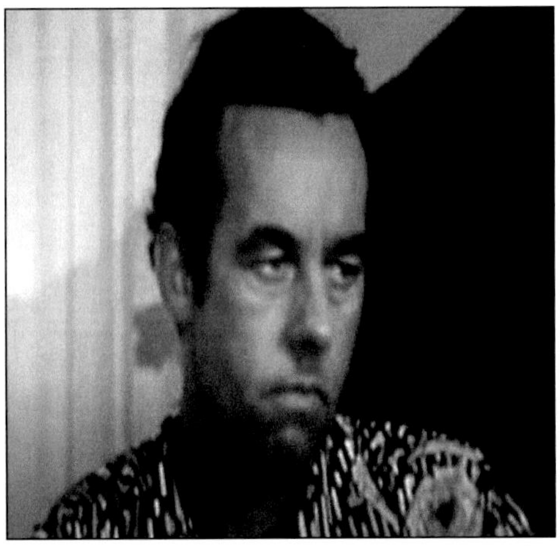

David Bufkin claimed to be a veteran of the Korean and Vietnam wars as well as working for the CIA. In December 1975, Bufkin was reportedly recruiting US mercenaries for Angola. Gary Acker was recruited by Bufkin around that time.

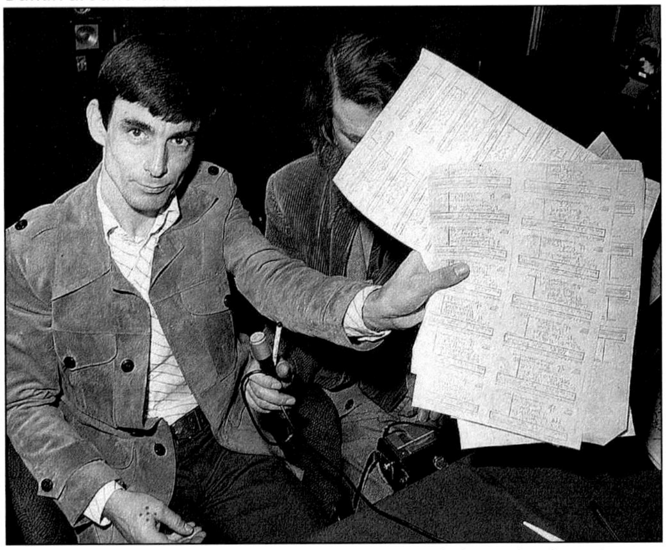

John Banks was a former British paratrooper and claimed to have been recruited by the CIA as well as US Army Special Forces in Vietnam. His PMC Security Advisory Services (SAS) was the main recruiter of British mercenaries for Angola.

would remain in Angola for five months, and recruits were to be paid according to their marital situation and if they had a wife and children. The pay scale was as follows:

- Private – $500 per month
- Sergeant – $650
- Second Lieutenant – $800
- Captain – $1,400
- Major – $2,500

In addition to this salary, $100 per month was to be awarded if the soldier was married, and $50 was to be paid monthly for each child. Travel costs were estimated at $200,000, medical costs at $50,000, bonuses at $100,000, and living allowances while in Angola at $75,000. Castro, himself, was to be paid $25,000.[36]

As was the case for Giscard and a 1,000-strong mercenary army, the Portuguese programme to recruit 300 men never materialised. One sergeant arrived on 1 January 1976, 12 others arrived four weeks later, and with the FNLA encountering severe difficulties and under pressure from the MPLA any further programme looked doomed to fail. There was, nevertheless, to be another twist in the mercenary tale: while the 13 Portuguese recruits returned to Lisbon without ever setting foot in Angola, Roberto had taken things into his own hands and had put the wheels in motion to build a mercenary army and to fund it with money given to him by the CIA in the scope of IA/FEATURE. Comprised mainly of former British soldiers, the actions of a few of them brought the CIA's operations in Angola to a hasty end and sullied even further the reputation of so-called 'soldiers of fortune'.

British Mercenaries in Angola: The John Banks Connection

Born on 15 November 1945, John Banks was the son of a serviceman in the Royal Army Medical Corps (RAMC) attached to the Airborne Forces and though born in the military town of Aldershot, Hampshire, UK, before the age of 10, Banks had lived in Egypt and Cyprus as his father was posted abroad. At 14 years old Banks showed an interest in joining the Royal Navy, but after a short time working as a labourer on a building site, on 2 September 1962 he signed up to join the army at its recruiting office in Reading and was sent to Maida Barracks in Aldershot, Hampshire for basic training with the Parachute Regiment. Excelling during training and finishing as the top recruit in his platoon, the 5'8 Banks (serial number 23933461) was assigned to the 2nd Battalion of the Parachute Regiment where he ended up in D Company, the pathfinder unit of the brigade whose job it was to be dropped into enemy territory and to set up landing zones for other units arriving later. Though never used to perform this role, in 1964 the 2nd Battalion was sent to Aden where its mission was to patrol the border with the Yemen and to stop rebels from operating. Here, Banks served at Cap Badge Ridge during the so-called Radfan Campaign (January-May 1964), and in December of that year he learnt he was being sent to Borneo. During a stopover in Singapore, he formed a friendship with Cecil Martin 'Satch' Fortuin, a South African later sentenced by judges at the Luanda Trial to 24 years in prison for his role as a mercenary.

After six weeks of intensive training at the Jungle Warfare School at Johor Bahru in the then Malaya and a tour of Borneo spent in the Sarawak Mountains, in February 1967 Banks was first posted to the Trucial Oman States in the Persian Gulf and again to Aden. During this tour when, once again, he met up with Fortuin, Banks claims to have been injured by a grenade thrown by a rebel from a window. A tour in Germany ended with Banks getting married in July 1968, but as Britain began to pull its soldiers out of Asian and Middle Eastern conflicts at the end of the 1960s, Banks knew that his time in the British Army was nearing an end. In June 1969, he was called into the OC's office where he was informed that his services were "no longer required".

The "civvy street" on which Banks found himself on after leaving the army did not offer much for men trained only to jump out of aircraft flying at 22,000 feet, or qualified to fire machine guns, mortars and rocket launchers. After two weeks on the 'dole', Banks's longing to continue soldiering brought him firstly to turning down the possibility of joining the Australian Army, but then trying to join the US Army due to their ongoing involvement in the Vietnam War. Though Banks states in his autobiography that the British did not rate US forces highly as fighting units, he was told that there was one good unit to join and that it was the Green Berets. At the time, it was possible for ex-British paratroopers and former Special Air Service (SAS) to join the US forces by applying at the US Embassy in London rather than flying to the United States to enlist. Invited for an interview with the US military attaché at the embassy in Grosvenor Square, a week later Banks was informed that he was now a sergeant in the US 5th Special Forces.

Banks was told that he was to be posted to Baden Baden in Germany for training and that after a year he would be sent to Vietnam to serve in the 7th Group. Taking the Oath of Allegiance to the United States, just a short time after arriving in Germany and after a trip back to the UK to arrange moving his wife and son abroad, Banks was once more called to the US Embassy in London. He was handed a file with a photo on the front cover that Banks immediately identified as showing his brother. Reportedly a mercenary having served with Jean Schramme's 10 Commando during the Congo Crisis,[37] on leaving Katanga this elder brother named Roger was now said to be running arms and ammunition into the Viet-Cong in the Mekong Delta. Because of this, Banks was informed that it was not possible for him to remain as a serving member of the US military. The next stage in Banks's then 25-year life was being offered the opportunity to smuggle people out of East Germany into West Germany. A lucrative offer as Banks was to be paid £1,500 per trip into the communist state, this job that Banks claimed was being bankrolled by the CIA involved recruiting former British soldiers and acquiring the tools and weapons needed to cut through fences and to ward off attacks from East German guards. Though the German assignment brought Banks into contact with the world of European mercenaries through a meeting with Charles Masy at the Café Renaissance in Brussels,[38] the possibility that Banks would end up in a gulag or dead convinced him after trips back and forth across the English Channel that the risks far outweighed any financial benefit.

In June 1970 a new opportunity for Banks to earn a large sum of money very quickly came in the shape of Watchguard International Ltd., a private military company (PMC) set up by David Stirling, the founder of the SAS, and Lieutenant Colonel John Woodhouse in 1965. A PMC well known amongst ex-paras and SAS with offices in Sloane Street, Watchguard was a unit that performed various mercenary operations throughout Africa and the Middle East. Stirling explained to Banks that Watchguard needed a radio operator for a contract in the Middle East and that he would be paid £5,000 for one night's work. Told to report to the Prince's Court Hotel in London's Knightsbridge one week later, what Banks did not know at the time was that he was being recruited for a mission called the Hilton Assignment, an operation financed by Umaral al-Shalhi, a millionaire supporter of Libyan King Idris. In 1969, Idris was deposed by Colonel Muammar Gaddafi and the plan was to overthrow Gaddafi's regime and return Idris to the throne.

Also involving Peter McAleese (another former British mercenary who was to serve in Angola in 1976) and a Frenchman named "Leon",[39] the plan was for a team of 25 men to travel to Tripoli aboard a converted naval launch boat named the *Conquistador III*. Once the launch had landed, the men were to proceed to a prison nicknamed the "Hilton" in which political opponents to Gaddafi's regime were being held. On their release, these prisoners would start an armed movement whose intention was to mount a counter-coup. Bank's own role consisted of travelling to Bari in Italy to join the launch, then to continue on to Plod in the former Yugoslavia to collect a batch of Czech-made weapons. Though Banks made it as far as Trieste in Italy, by then MI6 had got wind of the operation and put pressure on the Italian secret service the *Servizio Informazione Difesa* (SID) to arrest anyone suspected of having any sort of involvement. Banks spent a week in jail but was then deported to the UK. By all accounts, it appeared that the British government feared reprisals from Gaddafi should the identity of the mercenaries be discovered. At the time, Gaddafi was also considered to be pro-West.

Taking inspiration from Watchguard, Banks then set up his own security company and named it Agency Bodyguards. The company saw a certain degree of success supplying security for one of London's biggest casinos, the Victoria Sporting Club, but it ran into trouble when Banks attempted to win contracts in the Middle East. He sent two ex-paratrooper friends to Tel Aviv to protect rich Jewish businessmen, but before long they had developed a side-line and were organising snatch operations against Arabs in Jordan and Lebanon. MOSSAD learnt of these operations and the two men were arrested and deported back to the UK. One was Derek 'Brummie' Barker, a mercenary sentenced to death and executed in Angola in July 1976.

In another twist to a varied career, in February 1971 Banks claims to have been sent to Saigon and then to Da Nang where he joined a small group of British mercenaries sent into North Vietnam to carry out demolition, sabotage, kidnapping and assassination. A year later, he was recruited as a mercenary on behalf of a Kurd separatist movement fighting against the Iraqi government, and then was to be found driving articulated lorries full of cannabis on routes throughout Europe and the Middle East. Yet again, Banks was inspired to set up another business, and in 1974, he set up a haulage company called Trans-Asian Express. Banks's latest venture came to a grinding halt in July 1975 after running into financial difficulties.

Banks's next move was to call a meeting of old friends including Frank Perren with the idea of creating another security company that, this time, would be directly based on the Watchguard model. Within hours of discussing strategy with Perren, a former Royal Marine and member of the Special Boat Service (SBS), it was agreed that the best method to recruit the type of men needed to perform mercenary work was to appeal to them by placing adverts in two British newspapers, the *Daily Mirror* and the *Daily Mail*. The adverts reading "Ex-Commandos, paratroopers, SAS troopers wanted for interesting work abroad. Ring Camberley 33456", Banks was inundated with enquiries from Vietnam veterans, ex-Foreign Legionnaires, former Rhodesian SAS troopers as well as former soldiers from South Africa, France, Belgium, Italy and Germany. Within days, Banks had hundreds of former soldiers on his books, and even had to ask an old friend to man the phones at the office in Camberley. This turned out to be Dave Tomkins, one of the drivers for Trans-Asian Express; a professional burglar and an explosives expert. Tomkins, too, would end up as a mercenary in Angola, but was not captured and did not stand trial in Luanda.

After only 48 hours as head of the still unnamed company, Banks claims that he was contacted by two former SAS majors who had worked with him on the Hilton Assignment. At a meeting held at the headquarters of the SAS in Hereford, Banks was then informed that he was going to be offered two contracts: the first involved a plan to overthrow Nigeria's general Gowon, the man who had defeated Biafran rebels in 1970; and the second was a plan for as many as a thousand mercenaries to invade Rhodesia from Zambia. Whereas only the first contract was retained by Banks's contacts, the second called for Banks to raise three SAS-type squadrons and a logistical squadron. The plan was for these squadrons to enter Rhodesia from Zambia and carry out sabotage operations, and to confront Rhodesian forces. Recruits were to be paid £150 per week plus bonuses for successful operations and that each man was to be insured for £25,000.

The next phase consisted of selecting men to form squadrons of 110 men and setting up a command structure within each squadron. An OC, a 2 i/c were chosen as well as two former SAS Warrant Officers (Peter McAleese being one of them), then Banks planned to fill the ranks of the squadron by holding a series of interviews at the Regent Centre Hotel (probably the Regent Palace Hotel) near to Piccadilly Circus. It was just before interviews were held on Tuesday 27 May 1975 that Banks and his associate settled on the name International Security Organisation (ISO). With 90 potential recruits gathered in the hotel's Devonshire Room, almost all were former soldiers and a number of them were later to be recruited for Angola: Jamie McCandless (15 years SAS), Sammy Copeland (Parachute Regiment), Chris Dempster, Tony Boddy and Satch Fortuin. A second meeting was held on Thursday 29 May at the same hotel and it attracted almost as many applicants as the first. However, many South Africans, Rhodesians and British nationals left the room after learning that the target was Rhodesia, and during the following days Banks received death threats from supporters of Ian Smith's regime. One incident involved Banks being shot while in another two former RAF pilots even said that they planned to fly over Banks's offices in Camberley and bomb them. Two weeks after the interviews, about 200 men had been chosen to form squadrons comprising six officers, 34 sergeants and 45 troopers. These squadrons were broken down into 15 platoons with each one containing four men. Former Marine Commando and Foreign Legionnaire Mike Johnson was appointed Major while the RSM was to be Sammy Copeland.

Though the men had been told to prepare to fly out in August 1975, in late July Banks received notice that a group of 17 men were to fly to Zambia to discuss plans with guerrilla leaders. Johnson and McAleese were among those chosen to go, and on 27 July they joined 15 others at the Skyline Hotel at London Heathrow ready for a departure on the following Monday. As the men had been told that ISO would cover all their expenses at the hotel, it was inevitable that things would get out of hand as, in Banks's words, the men "drank like fish, ate like Henry VIII, and screwed like Casanova". Fights broke out between the mercenaries, and an ex-Congo Belgian mercenary threw four ladies in evening dress into the swimming pool. Events taking place at the Skyline Hotel naturally led to the British press becoming interested. Newspaper reporters were quick to sense a story and the next day Banks received a call from the British Special Branch telling him that his group of mercenaries must be removed from the hotel as early as possible. The behaviour of the mercenaries at the Skyline was enough for the mission to be cancelled and for the mercenaries to be dismissed.

Bringing to a close the Rhodesia contract, in early August 1975, the name International Security Organisation was scrapped due to its lack of credibility, but Banks had not yet finished with the recruitment of mercenaries nor with adventures into Africa. Sitting down one evening with Dave Tomkins, a new company bearing a new name saw the light of day. This one, Security Advisory Services (SAS) was chosen for its obvious connection to the British special forces unit that carried the same initials.[40]

The Belford -Taylor Connection

The story of how over a hundred British mercenaries came to be fighting in a war seemingly disconnected from the Anglosphere starts in late 1975 when four veterans of the so-called 'Troubles' in Northern Ireland named "Nick" Hall,[41] Costas Georgiou, Charles Christodoulou, and Michael Wainhouse were seeking to brighten up what they considered as a dull existence on 'civvy street'. The four men working as plasterers on building sites and scanning the newspapers for a war in which they could ply a trade learnt with the British Parachute Regiment, it was Hall who suggested that they look towards Angola.[42] Having identified that the FNLA was the side that best represented their own anti-communist view of the world, what remained was to make contact with Roberto so that they could offer their services. It was through Martin Meredith of *The Sunday Times* that Hall learnt that the FNLA had an official representative in the UK. Based in Leeds, and a former PT instructor in the British Army, Donald Belford had become involved with the FNLA as early as 1970 when he acted as a medic attending FNLA soldiers wounded in fighting with Portuguese forces. Equally a member of the South African Friendship Association, Belford promised to put Hall in contact with Roberto while Hall supplied Belford with a phone number belonging to Costas Georgiou.[43]

Like Hall, Georgiou had spent time in prison for committing criminal offences in Northern Ireland during active tours of the province. Hall was convicted of taking part in the brutal assault of a civilian and trying to sell weapons to the Ulster Volunteer Force (UVF), a Protestant paramilitary group, while Georgiou held up a post office using a weapon given to him by the British Army. He then threatened to kill the prosecuting officer and was sent to the 'Glasshouse' for five years. Having also been identified as someone who fired up to 26 shots at protesters in Londonderry on 'Bloody Sunday',[44] Georgiou was a highly competitive individual picking up regimental awards for being the best machine-gunner and the best marksman during his time in training. These skills leading him to be appointed as a weapons instructor to the Ulster Defence Regiment (UDR), Georgiou's competiveness meant that he felt he should take the lead from Hall for the Angola adventure and deal directly with Belford. The chance came when Belford rang the then 23 year-old Greek-Cypriot towards the end of October 1975.[45] Leaving his parents' flat at 66 Kendal House, London, N1,[46] Georgiou then travelled to Leeds where he had arranged to meet Belford and one of his associates named Colin Taylor, a brash Londoner who presented himself as the European Security Officer for the FNLA.[47] Belford informed Georgiou that Roberto had accepted the four men's' offer of help but unfortunately only had funds to send one of them to Angola. Georgiou naturally taking up the offer for himself, Taylor then told Georgiou that he would have to prove his loyalty to the FNLA by attacking the MPLA's office in London.[48] The task was accepted by Georgiou, and on 6 November 1975 he and another of the group of ex-paratroopers headed for the offices of the Angolan Solidarity Committee, a group of individuals producing propaganda for the MPLA out of the Mozambique and Guinea Information Centre on number 12 Little Newport Street near London's Leicester Square.[49] Though the attack resulted only in causing a small amount of fire damage to the offices, this proved to be enough to demonstrate that Georgiou and his group were loyal to Roberto's cause.[50] Another motivation for Georgiou was Taylor's mention that diamonds used to finance the FNLA's war effort were to be found in a bank vault in Carmona. Due to leave for Angola within a few days, according to Chris Dempster and Dave Tomkins, Georgiou met with his cohort in a bar in London's King's Cross area. Explaining to them that his name might be mentioned in newspaper reports, Georgiou announced that he was changing his name and would now be known as "Tony Callan".[51] On 28 November 1975, "Callan", along with Belford and Taylor flew to Belgium

Costas Georgiou alias "Colonel Tony Callan" is pictured here talking to FNLA recruits. As was the case with local villagers brought in to bolster the ranks of the MPLA, the recruits were poor farmers with no military experience.

on the first leg of a journey that would lead Georgiou to becoming Angola's most feared mercenary.

The three men arrived in Kinshasa on 2 December 1975 where they were given rooms at the Intercontinental Hotel. Though expecting to meet with Roberto, after three days Belford, Taylor and Callan flew to Negage in northern Angola to meet up with FNLA commanders. The town having been mostly deserted by the FNLA who feared the arrival of Cuban soldiers, Callan's time in Negage was spent acting as an assistant to Belford in the local hospital where the FNLA's war casualties were being treated.[52] Although Callan showed himself to be a competent medic at this time, he was soon to be brought into the conflict as a soldier when in Carmona he met Portuguese mercenaries fighting under Carlos Santos. Their telling Callan of how they had hijacked and commandeered Idi Amin's Cessna 310 as it refuelled in Carmona,[53] they also told him of rumours concerning the presence of 200 US mercenaries that had supposedly arrived in Angola in November.[54]

The photo taken during the same meeting with local recruits, as a former weapons instructor with the British Parachute Regiment Callan was well placed to transfer knowledge to men who had never held a rifle. Many of the FNLA's local recruits would fall victim to Callan's brutality.

While Belford and Taylor left Angola on 18 December 1975, the day after Gerald Ford announced that the US had no "military advisors" in Angola,[55] Callan woke on 29 December to find a Soviet T-34 tank only metres from where he was billeted. He realised that the FNLA had once again deserted the area, that he was alone, and that in some way he would have to escape from the advance of the Cuban/FAPLA forces. According to accounts, it was at this moment that Callan ceased to be a medic and became an active soldier fighting for the FNLA. Armed with an Uzi sub-machine gun, Callan escaped in a Volkswagen which he drove to Negage and began to organise a counterattack. Accompanied by two Portuguese mercenaries, Callan's next step was to encounter a force allegedly led by Victor Manuel Correia Fernandes.[56] A group of his men having been sent out as an advance party some three days before, the scene that greeted Fernandes once he had tracked them down was one of devastation. The advance party's T-34s had been destroyed as had their four Katyusha rocket launchers; 60 men lay dead and others lay dying; and Fernandes believed that his soldiers must have run into an enemy of 100 or more.[57] The reality was, though, that this carnage had been caused by Callan and two Portuguese mercenaries. They had caught the advance party's camp off-guard, and over the next few hours managed to destroy the enemy. During the battle, Callan proved himself to be lethal. Indeed, whereas the two Portuguese killed dozens using Belgian FALs, Callan's contribution consisted of firing 66mm anti-tank rockets at the T-34s and Katyushas.

As more reports appeared in the *Christian Science Monitor* of 1 January 1976 that 150 Americans including Special Forces were undergoing training for Angola at Fort Benning, Georgia,[58] on 5 January that year, Hall, Wainhouse and Christodoulou finally arrived in Kinshasa accompanied by Donald Taylor. Staying in

Peter McAleese was a former member of the British SAS. Recruited by John Banks in 1975, McAleese became overall commander of the FNLA's operations in Angola and would later serve in the Rhodesian SAS as well as the SADF. (Author's collection)

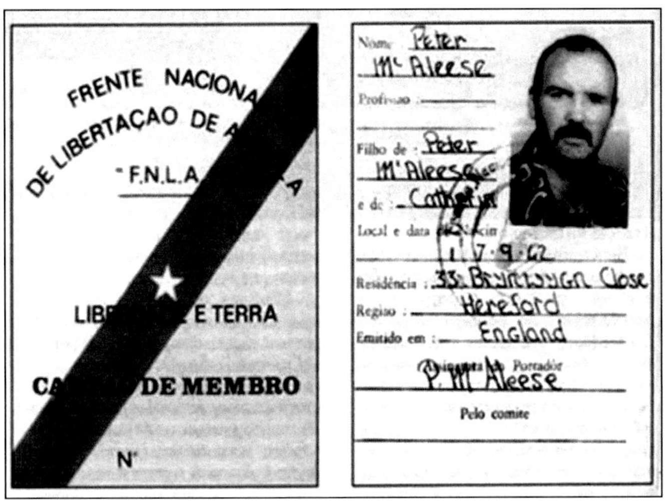

Peter McAleese's identity card. Note that his address is given as Hereford, the home of the British SAS. (Terry Aspinall)

rooms reserved for the FNLA at the Intercontinental with Callan, but still with no sign of Roberto, two days later the four met a CIA contractor who presented himself as "Jean-Pierre". Probably the CIA's agent referred to as Victor St. Martin in Jon Stockwell's account,[59] the meeting was held at the CIA's headquarters in the Binza district of Kinshasa.[60] A series of other meetings were held over the coming days; one involved Callan being threatened with death by UNITA's Daniel Chipenda; another involved Hall and Roberto who had finally made an appearance; but more significant was that which involved the CIA man and the leader of the FNLA. The Soviet build-up of weapons increasing day-by-day and the FNLA rapidly ceding any territory it held in northern Angola to the FAPLA, it was important that the FNLA appoint a new field commander. Within a matter of 48 hours, Costas Georgiou alias "Tony Callan" had become "Colonel Callan".

The Aspin – Banks – Hall Connection

If Leslie Aspin's biographical account were to be believed,[61] at different stages in his life he had been a cigarette and arms smuggler, a pilot, and an MI6 agent codenamed "Kovaks" who on the run from the Black September group, the IRA and a "handful of Mafia hit-men".[62] Dismissed as a Walter Mitty-like character by Peter McAleese in his autobiography first published in 1993,[63] due to Aspin's claims of having single-handedly killed four Palestinians out to kill him, there might, nonetheless be an element of truth in the tale of a 31-year-old who also claims to have played a major role in the 1972 *Claudia* Affair as a Libyan secret agent,[64] and who had links to the CIA.[65] Firstly, Aspin would have needed an extremely vivid imagination, and, secondly, his accounts have been given credence in a monograph written by former US government prosecutor and former US Army intelligence officer, John Loftus.[66] Writing with Australian journalist, Mark Aarons, Loftus describes how on Aspin's death in 1988 his family uncovered an employment contract with British Secret Services and that Aspin was linked to the Iran-Contra Affair. Indeed, it was Aspin who allegedly helped George Bush Snr. circumvent the Congressional ban on the US supporting Nicaraguan Contras.[67] Loftus and Aaron also state that Aspin was a former member of the SAS. Lastly, Aspin is said to have worked with Syrian Monzer al-Kassar, an arms dealer who had been recruited by MI6 and who was also involved in the Iran-Contra Affair.[68] During this episode of Aspin's life, the name Larry Katz was to turn up. Katz was an employee of the US Drugs Enforcement Agency (DEA) who knew that the British had recruited al-Kassar due to his time running the DEA's London office,[69] and it was Katz that Aspin turned to when confirmation was needed that Hall now represented the FNLA when the latter returned to London in January 1976.[70] Another US official said to be facilitating mercenary recruitment in the UK was the assistant US Army attaché in London, Major James Leonard.[71]

As for Operation IA/FEATURE, Ford's plans to support the FNLA and UNITA had received a blow that came in the shape of the Tunney Amendment of December 1975. An amendment to the Defense Appropriations Act of 1976 and sponsored by California Senator John V. Tunney, it effectively ended funding for covert operations in Angola. Ford signing the act and its becoming law on 9 February 1976, funds for any future operations to hire mercenaries would have to come from other sources. It was fortunate for the CIA, then, that over the years Roberto had amassed a fortune due to his annual stipend from the CIA, business dealings in the Cabindan enclave which started in the early 1950s, and funding from Gaddafi and French secret services.

With Hall now acting as Roberto's driver, bodyguard, and having been promoted to the rank of Major in the FNLA, on 9 January 1976 Hall drove his employer back to Kinshasa leaving Callan to organise what remained of a beleaguered FNLA. Their having witnessed drunken Zairian soldiers along the way and Roberto making disparaging remarks about the quality of the FNLA's allies, Roberto's conversation turned to the question of how much it would cost to employ more British soldiers and bring them to Angola. The figure given by Hall being $1,000 per man, Roberto rapidly calculated that he could afford to bring an entire battalion of the Parachute Regiment to Angola for around $1 million. As it was, Roberto's plans to recruit British soldiers began modestly. The same evening, effectively, Roberto handed Hall $25,000 in cash with which to hire the first 25 mercenaries. The money made up of consecutively numbered $100 notes, it was clear that it had been especially printed for the CIA.[72]

On 12 January 1976, Nick Hall made his way back to London carrying proof that he represented Roberto and that he was accredited to act in the group's interest. Shortly after his arrival, Hall then contacted Charley Christodoulou and, in turn, was told to contact Michael Wright, an ex-Rhodesian SAS trooper who

B.A.B. NORWICH LTD.
(SECURITY ADVISORY SERVICES)

RECRUITMENT

44 ROSE LANE
NORWICH, NORFOLK
ENGLAND
Telephone: NORWICH (0603) 613581

CONFIDENTIAL

NAME: .... TEL NO: ....

ADDRESS: RESIDENTIAL ....

BUSINESS ....

MILITARY QUALIFICATIONS:

AIRBORNE: .... MAP READING (Air photo) MEDICS QUAL: ....

SMALLARMS, TYPES: .... MECHANICS, TYPE: .....

BOATS, TYPE: ....

RADIO: OPS: TYPE: ....

SUPPORT ARMS, TYPE: ... LANGUAGES: ....

DEMOLITIONS: ....

RANK ON DISCHARGE: ....

PILOT, AIRCRAFT TYPE:

ACTIVE SERVICE: (Theatre, Length, Job Type) ....

REMARKS: (Special Qualifications) ....

MEDICAL: Drug Allergies, Inoculations, Type & Date ....

PASSPORT NO & COUNTRY: ....

NEXT OF KIN: (Name & Address) ....

....TEL NO: ....

DESCRIPTION: Height .... Weight ....

In early 1976, John Banks, Leslie Aspin and "Ginger" Best (real name John Chownes) set up offices in Norwich. Using the name B.A.B, the new company was an incarnation of Security Advisory Services. (Terry Aspinall)

B.A.B. NORWICH LTD.
(SECURITY ADVISORY SERVICES)

RECRUITMENT

44 ROSE LANE
NORWICH, NORFOLK
ENGLAND
Telephone: NORWICH (0603) 613581

CONFIDENTIAL

FULL NAME: ....

ADDRESS: ....

DATE OF BIRTH: .... TEL NO: .... NATIONALITY: ....

PROPOSED BENEFICIARY
OR
NEXT OF KIN

TEL NO: ....

NAME: ....

ADDRESS: ....

RELATIONSHIP: ....

OWN BANK. Account No: ....

NAME OF BANK: ....

ADDRESS OF BANK: ....

HEALTH DECLARATION:

I am now in good health and am not suffering any physical infirmaties.

I hereby nominate as my Administrators:-

....

....

I am/not willing to work in any part of world.

SIGNED: .... DATE: ....

WITNESS: .... NAME: ....

ADDRESS: ....

The naming of the proposed beneficiary and next of kin was a standard mention on recruitment forms for the British Army and for recruitment with B.A.B. (Terry Aspinall)

would later serve in Angola. Another former British serviceman Hall met was Daniel Aitkin. A member of the Special Boat Service, Aitkin would also make his way to Kinshasa later that month. According to Dempster and Tomkins's account, with Hall finding it difficult to find suitable candidates for recruitment, he then contacted journalist Tony Geraghty who advised Hall to get in touch with Philip Woodley, an insurance agent employed to insure British mercenaries recruited by a certain John Banks for operations linked to Banks's ISO.[73]

Just after midnight on 17 January 1976, Banks met up with Dave Tomkins in a nightclub in Camberley. Though Tomkins was not hoping for much from Banks given the recent failure of the incarnation of ISO, Security Advisory Services also in financial trouble, Banks informed him that he had met Hall and that SAS had secured a contract to provide 25 mercenaries. Banks was to be paid £200 for every man he could provide, the mercenaries themselves were to be paid £150 per week, and their role was to train FNLA troops.[74] Just a couple of hours later, Banks and Tomkins took a taxi to the Tower Hotel in central London where they met Leslie Aspin and Frank Perren. Aspin, who had been present when ISO was recruiting mercenaries for operations in Rhodesia, had been employed by Banks to help with mercenary recruitment and to provide his own brand of expertise. This came in the form of carrying out background checks on Hall and verifying that he genuinely represented the FNLA, which Aspin was able to do through Larry Katz at the US Embassy.[75] The early hours of 17 January 1976 were eventful in that Hall turned up at 4 a.m. to present the Angolan situation and the military position of the FNLA. The recruiters were told that the FNLA possessed an array of modern weaponry including tanks and armoured cars, but that unfortunately what was missing were professional soldiers who could train local recruits how to use them.

With Banks, Aspin and Perren convinced by Hall, the next step was how to find 25 mercenaries who would be ready to leave within a matter of days.[76] Security surrounding the nature of ISO and SAS meant that the names of Banks's previously recruited army were to be found in a safe in Norwich, so the first batch of mercenaries for Angola would have to be drawn from those known personally and whom could be contacted straightaway. The first man contacted was Jamie McCandless, a former member of the Special Air Service; he then contacted Tony Boddy and Sammy Copeland. Explosives expert Dave Tomkins had already put his name forward, and he contacted Chris Dempster, a "first-class" mechanic according to their joint account.[77] Another who was recruited on 17 January was Peter McAleese. According to his own account, Nick Hall phoned McAleese who was residing in Hereford, the home of the SAS. McAleese was told to meet up at the Tower Hotel in London the following day.[78] When McAleese arrived at the hotel found just a short walk from Tower Bridge, he was greeted by the sight of around 24 people stood in one room, room 332. McAleese had brought along his cousin Tommy, a former British paratrooper and men such as Derek John "Brummie" Barker, Tony Boddy, 'Fuzz' Hussey, Mike Johnson, Jamie McCandless, Sammy Copeland and Andrew McKenzie were also waiting to receive a first payment and a plane ticket to

Kinshasa. Within a month all would be dead apart from Barker and McKenzie. Both were executed by firing squad in Luanda some six months later.

Twenty-four hours from Kinshasa

The second advance party now recruited and flights for Kinshasa *via* Brussels and Athens arranged for 8.30 in the evening of Sunday, 18 January, the men congregated once more at the Tower Hotel where 16 double rooms had been reserved under the name the 'Manchester Sporting Club'. Given hastily manufactured travel documents prepared by Frank Perren, the men were briefed by Hall who informed them that their base in Angola was at São (or San) Salvador, a few miles from the Zairian border with Angola. Here, the men were told, they would meet the C/O (Callan), and also a number of Portuguese mercenaries. If injured, they were told that first-class medical attention awaited them and even that USAF planes were available should they need to be taken back to the UK for treatment.[79]

Following what appeared to be a good deal of cooperation from British border control officers – some of the men did not have passports[80] – the DC-10 carrying the mercenaries finally touched down at N'Dolo Airport in Kinshasa in the evening of 19 January. Driven to the Palace Hotel to await the arrival of Roberto, the FNLA leader finally arrived accompanied by well-armed bodyguards and a "white man" assumed to be one of the CIA's paymasters due to his North American accent. The man in question being a Canadian named Douglas Newby according to McAleese,[81] the next stop was a trip across Kinshasa to Roberto's villa where the men were given arms and uniforms, most of them of Belgian origin.

As the mercenary group would soon discover, the 200 miles of pot-holed roads and the abundant populations of mosquitoes were the very least of their problems. Effectively, when reaching the FNLA's headquarters at São Salvador, they realised that the promise of being handed up-to-date equipment was one that was never going to be fulfilled. Their suspicions should have been raised at Roberto's Kinshasa villa. Indeed, in an interview for George Washington University, Tomkins spoke of how the mercenaries were given boots without laces, no belts to hold their trousers up, and a "motley collection" of camouflage clothing.[82] Things were far worse at São Salvador. The streets were littered with detritus of all kinds, small children played in the dust in front of decaying buildings once tended and occupied by Portuguese settlers, and what is more Callan was waiting to greet the latest recruits for the FNLA. After the mercenaries' new O/C had given them a dressing down due to their generally civilian appearance, the men were taken on a tour of the house revealing that Callan's forces possessed a wide array of armaments that in turn revealed exactly who was sponsoring who in the Angolan Civil War. In addition to the Uzi sub-machine guns, British Sterling and Sten guns, a large selection of pistols including Walther PPKs and PPs, Berettas, Smith & Wessons, Colts and Star automatics. Stockwell confirming that IA/FEATURE weapons were being used by the mercenaries,[83] there was also a large selection of Soviet weapons captured from the MPLA. The following photograph shows a small assortment of the weapons recovered and presented as

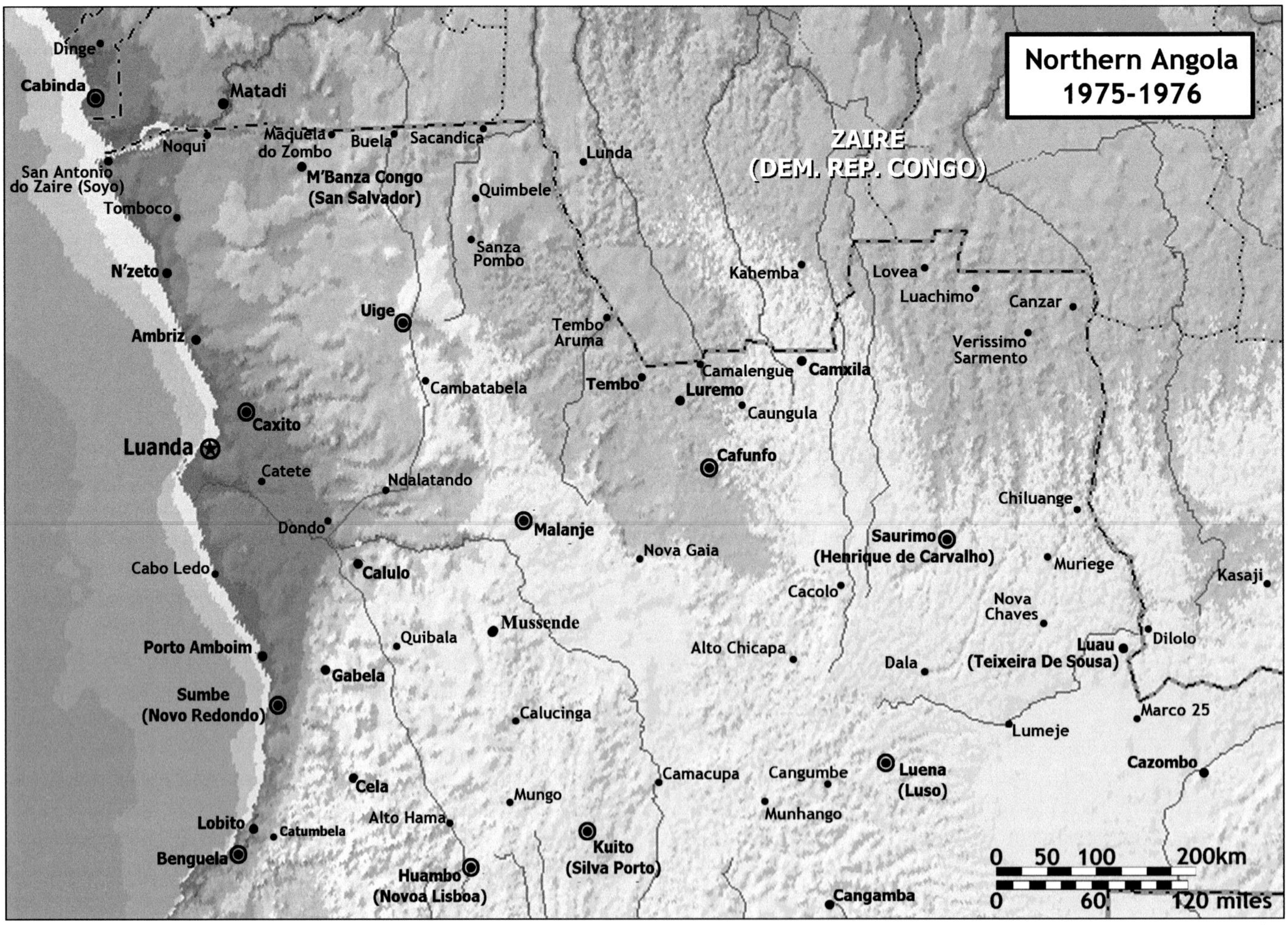

Map of northern Angola: the CIA's British mercenaries were foremost operating in the area between Ambriz on the coast of the Atlantic Ocean, and Quimbela on the border to Zaire. (Map by Tom Cooper)

Total number of Weapons and Materiel delivered to FNLA and UNITA by CIA

1. Heavy weapons	
SA7 'GRAIL' SAMs	26
120 mm. mortars	14
106 mm. recoilless rifles (probably M40)	14
4.2 inch mortars (probably M30)	38
3.5 inch rocket-launchers (probably M8)	90
82 mm. mortars (probably M37)	20
81 mm. mortars (probably M252)	80
60 mm. mortars (probably M224)	319
.50 cal. heavy machine guns (probably M2)	20
RPG-7 grenade launchers	25

2. Machine guns, rifles and individual weapons	
M72 LAWS 66 mm.	4,120
M79 40 mm. grenade launchers	410
.30 cal. light machine guns (LMG)	240
7.62 mm. light machine guns (LMG)	124
7.62 mm rifles	7,771
.30 cal. carbines	12,215
9 mm. submachine guns	66
9 mm. pistols	150
Hand grenades	1,170

3. Ammunition	
HE mortar 120 mm. rounds	3,430
HEAT recoilless rifle 106 mm. rounds	1,974
HEP recoilless rifle 106 mm. rounds	1,800
HE 4.2 inch mortar	2,549
WP 4.2 inch mortar	100
ILLUM 4.2 inch mortar	100
Rocket launcher rounds 3.5 inch	1,649
HE 90 mm. rounds	2,456
HEAT 90 mm. rounds	2,032
HE 81 mm. mortar rounds	9,743
WP 81 mm. mortar rounds	810
ILLUM 81 mm. mortar rounds	249
HE 60 mm. mortar rounds	19,821
WP 60 mm. mortar rounds	1,760
ILLUM 60 mm. mortar rounds	490
M79 40 mm. rounds	108,758

4. Miscellaneous	
PRC-25/27 radios	200
ANGRC-9 radios	20
RF-301 radios	10
TRA-921 radios	49
Medical supplies in lbs.	1,800

Adapted from a list supplied in Stockwell, pp.281-282

Callan gives orders to two FNLA soldiers. The gun mounted in this Land Rover is a DShK 38/46 12.7mm heavy machine gun with anti-aircraft sights. (Author's collection)

evidence at the Luanda Trial of June 1976.

The mercenaries' day was typical of what might be expected in any structured military outfit. Reveille was given at 6 a.m., uniforms had to be worn when on duty, the officers' mess was separated from that of the NCO's and the lower ranks, and weapons had to be cleaned to await inspection. It was during one of the first inspections that Callan's extremely violent nature became apparent to the British recruits. Whether this anger was borne from frustration at not having sufficient, trained manpower to fight off Cuban advances into northern Angola is not known. What has been documented, nonetheless, is that black recruits rather than those who had just arrived bore the brunt of Callan's pathological rages. He and Michael Wainhouse took particular pleasure in handing out severe beatings to his own

List of equipment stocked at mercenary bases in São Salvador and Quiende

Around 30 vehicles including:
Bedford RL medium truck (UK)
Dodge personnel carrier (probably G-507) (USA)
Ferret Scout Car (USA)
Panhard VBL (France)
Panhard EBR (France)
Panhard M3/VTT armoured personnel carrier (France)
2 Land Rovers with 106mm M40 recoilless rifles mounted on rear
11 other Land Rovers (not in working order) (UK)
Magirus-Deutz truck (Probably Mercur) (West Germany)
Mercedes-Benz L3000 truck (West Germany)

Machine guns
DShK 38/46 12.7mm heavy machine gun
Goryunova SG-43 machine gun (Soviet Union)
M1919 .30 Browning machine guns (USA)
Kalashnikov AK-47 (Soviet Union)
STEN machine gun (UK)
Sterling machine gun (UK)
Uzi sub-machine guns (Israeli origin)
FN FAL rifles (Belgium)
M1 Carbines (USA)
M2 Carbines (USA)

Rocket Launchers / mortars
M79 Grenade launchers (USA)
M76 Grenade launchers (USA)
M72 LAW 66mm rocket launchers plus rockets (USA)
HEAT (High Explosive Anti-Tank) missiles
Two-inch mortars (no ammunition). Probably the Ordnance SBML (UK)

Pistols
Beretta M9 pistols (Italian origin)
Colt 45 pistols (USA)
Smith & Wesson .44 Magnum (USA)
Star BM automatic pistols (USA)
TOZ pistol. Probably the TOZ-35 or TOZ-55 (Soviet Union)
Walther PPK pistols (USA)
Walther PP pistols (USA)
Walther P38 pistols (USA)
Very pistols

Explosives
Bangalore torpedo
Chinese-made hand grenades (several boxes)
Cordtex detonating cord
Detonator No.27 – Lexpev (Soviet Union)
Gelegnite
Hayrick explosive charges
MUV – Lexpev igniters (Soviet Union)
POMZ-2 anti-personnel fragmentation mines (Soviet Union)
PRB BAC Anti-personnel mines (Belgium)
PRM-ATK-M3 -Lexpev anti-tank mines (Soviet Union)
TNT (1 kg blocks)

Other
CS gas canisters

Reported to have been captured from mercenary forces
RPG-7 anti-tank rocket launcher (Soviet Union)
Kalashnikov AKS-47 machine gun (Soviet Union)
Dragunov sniper rifle (Soviet Union)
PKM machine gun (Soviet Union)

From left to right: RPG-7 anti-tank rocket launcher, an AKS-47, a Dragunov sniper rifle and a PKM machine gun. (geopoliticalcyprus.org)

Callan was a competent soldier. He also turned out to be a psychopath. (SOF Magazine)

forces for even the pettiest of crimes, and woe betide anyone suspected of being an enemy soldier. After the customary beating and mistreatment, the unfortunate would be summarily executed and then thrown off the Quiende bridge. In fact this bridge became something of a favourite destination for the disposal of bodies, especially those fighting for and not against the FNLA. Callan's cousin 'Charley' Christodoulou (aka 'Kebab Charley' and 'Shotgun Charley') boasted that he, Callan and Wainhouse alone had killed 167 FNLA recruits by either throwing them off the bridge when alive or after a beating. Another method of killing black recruits was testing weapons on them. As well as testing the power of Christodoulou's shotgun on an innocent FNLA recruit,[84] another poor unfortunate just happened to be closest to Callan when the time came for testing a .44 Magnum.[85] Both incidences producing predictable results, a third local had the misfortune of trying to enlist in the FNLA already armed with a small pistol. Callan being convinced that the man had been sent along to assassinate him, the local Angolan was immediately placed under arrest. Later that day he was "taken on a one-way trip to the bridge".[86] Sammy Copeland also seemed to take great pleasure in terrorising local blacks. As the group's Regimental Sergeant Major, the power his position gave him went straight to his head: on one occasion, Copeland could be seen marching Angolans before him shouting 'Viva la Sammy'.[87] With chaos everywhere around them, it did not take long for discord to appear between a group seemingly loyal to Callan, and another loyal to McAleese.

Before Callan and his cohort had time to turn their attention to their fellow mercenaries, and before relations between ex-Para and ex-SAS broke down completely, it was fortunate that on around 22 January Callan ordered McAleese to take charge of the coastal town of San Antonio do Zaire (now Soyo), some 150 miles from São Salvador and on the south bank of the Congo River estuary. The trip to Angola's most north-western tip was an eye-opener for McAleese and the six men who accompanied him (Barker, Johnson, Saunders, S. McPherson, Rennie and Tilsey). Flying above Angola in a Fokker Friendship piloted by a Portuguese and paid for by the CIA,[88] this was the first chance McAleese had had to survey the vast expanses of the Angolan bush and the network of scrub roads that linked each isolated village to its neighbour.

Roberto was to meet McAleese in San Antonio and he explained how he thought it was vital to hold out against the MPLA in the area.[89] The MPLA's Cuban support having reached between 10,000-12,000 soldiers on 22 January,[90] the zone was already under threat with Ambrizete (now N'Zeto) having been taken days before. If the MPLA managed to reach and gain control of Ambrizete, the FNLA would find itself confined to a small sector bordering Zaire. In the meantime, the *New York Times* reported that South Africa was withdrawing its forces to "non-operational" areas.[91] This would have the effect of the MPLA being able to

A Fokker F.27 of the Direcçao dos Transpotes Aéreos (DAT) was used to ferry supplies to São Salvador. The same type of aircraft was allegedly supplied by the CIA and served as transport for mercenaries inside Angola. This Fokker Friendship is pictured at Benguela Airport in Angola in the late 1960s. (Author's collection)

bolster forces in northern Angola and exert more pressure on Roberto's already thin resources in terms of manpower.

Mercenary Operations and the Maquela Massacre

With most activity being carried out in a triangular area covering Damba, São Salvador and Maquela (see Map 4), apart from an incident at the main FNLA garrison at Quiende on 21 January where there was a mini revolt by black soldiers, any goings-on were limited to making weapons and vehicles battle-ready or setting booby traps, planting mines and setting up defensive positions (especially around Maquela). This being partly due to the heavy rainfalls that occur in Angola between November and April each year, the first signs that direction confrontation with FAPLA/Cuban forces appeared when Callan received notice that they had taken Damba and that he should send reinforcements to Maquela as soon as possible. The plan was to send one group of FNLA/mercenary towards Quibocolo to act as an advance party while the remainder made its way to the FNLA base at Maquela. From here, the first group was to take up positions around the Rio Zardi Bridge and the second would make its way along the road (now the EN140 between Damba and Maquela) in order to find suitable higher ground from which an ambush could be launched. Whereas anti-personnel mines would be placed on one side of the road to entrap those attempting to shelter from firing from the hillside, the FAPLA/Cuban column would be attacked using M72 LAWs and the Panhard armoured car.[92]

The mercenary convoy of around 30 vehicles leaving São Salvador in the early morning of 23 January, it soon became evident that the climatic conditions and the landscape were going to pose more than a sizeable problem. The only principal route lying between São Salvador and Maquela being no more than a dirt track that ended some 30 kms west of the village of Cuimba, not only was visibility reduced to almost nothing by torrential downpours, the rain-soaked tracks offered little grip even for Land Rovers or Bedford trucks. The efforts to make any meaningful headway severely hampered by deep,

The village of Cuimba lies between São Salvador and Maquela do Zombo and lies northwest of Quibocolo and Damba. (AEJE)

São Salvador in northern Angola. This town was used as the main base for British mercenaries in January and February 1976. (AEJE)

Pictured in 1972, Maquela do Zombo was an important staging point between Damba and the Zairian border. Just outside the village, in February 1976 it was the scene of the Maquela Massacre. (Mapio.net)

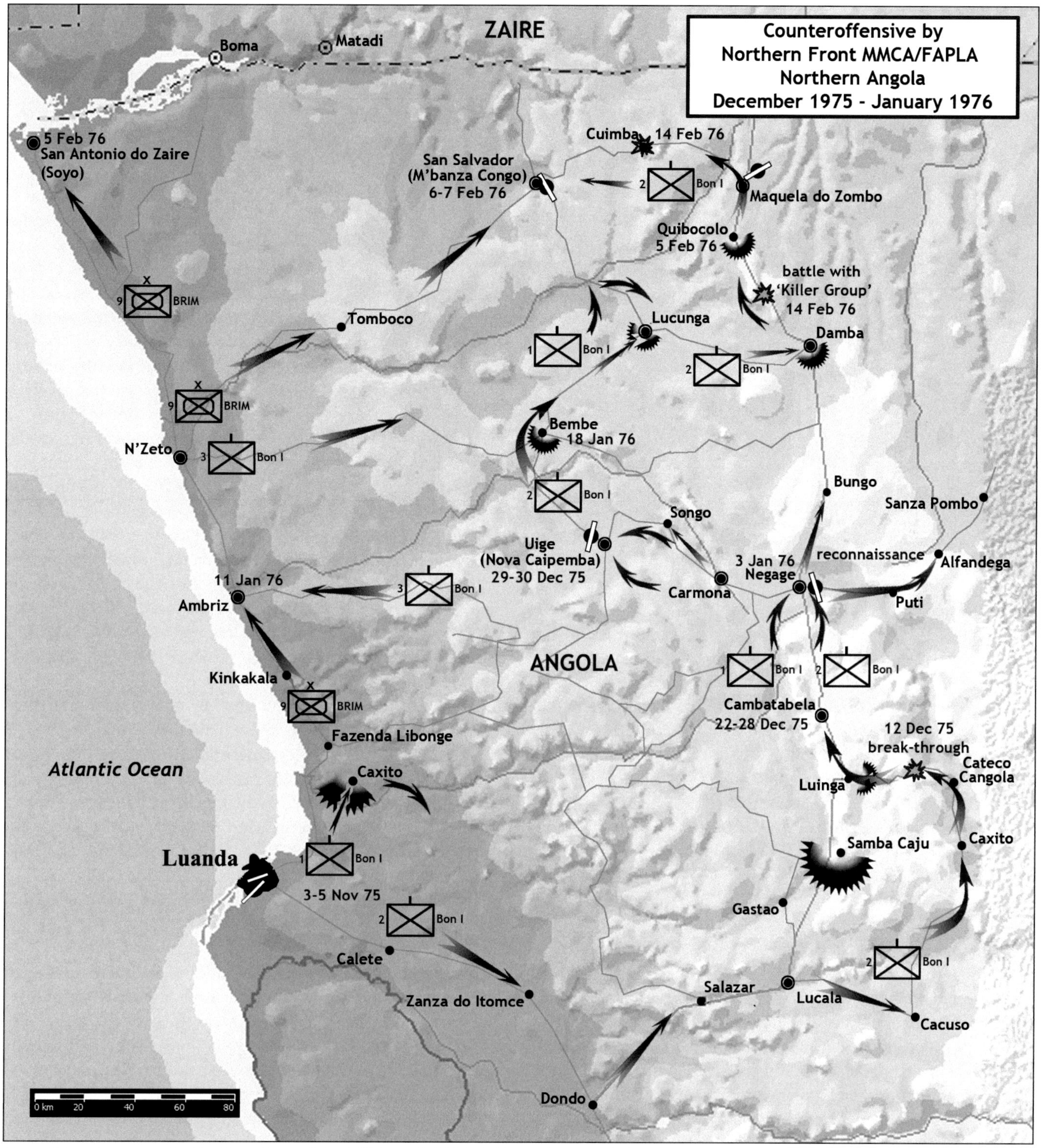

Map of the advance by the Northern Front of the MMCA and FAPLA, in November 1975-February 1976. Of particular interest is the eastern prong of this operation: conducted by the Cuban-advised 2 Bon I – reinforced by the 1 Bon I, 3 Bon I, 4 Bon I and a number of smaller FAPLA units as and when necessary – this followed the principle of the 'Auftragstaktik', developed by the German Army during the 1940s. It was this advance that eventually resulted in the showdown with the CIA-recruited mercenaries, in the area between Damba and Cuimba, in early and mid-February 1976. (Map by Tom Cooper)

muddy ruts, another problem was the wind that blew the tarpaulin covers off of the vehicles leaving men and munitions exposed to the elements.

Though the exact dates on which events took place may differ according to which source is used to gather information, and Cuban sources appearing to amalgamate two different incidents involving mercenaries, it is clear that by the final week of January Cuban forces had made steady progress into FNLA-held territory and were planning to advance on Maquela, one of the last FNLA strongholds that lay between Damba and the Zairian border. The roads on which the Cubans advanced being far more suitable for heavy military vehicles, the 2nd Battalion of the FAPLA forces under Major Gonzalo del Valle Céspedes had made its way up country to Negage from where it was to proceed 250 kilometres northwards along the EN140 road. The column possessing infantry, T-34s, BM-21 rocket launchers, and 120mm, 82mm and 75mm batteries first spotted Callan's five-man ambush party just outside Damba. Their being out of reach of shelling provided by

Mercenaries inspect an abandoned or captured BM-21 just outside Damba at the end of January 1976.

that they had been recruited for non-combat duties. There were even civilians amongst them: William Brooks had been employed as a driver as had David Heaton and Harry Webb.

After having separated 23 non-combatants from the recently arrived and inviting them to walk back to Kinshasa, the 70 remaining were billeted in different accommodation and told to await orders. Around midday another message was received informing Callan that a Cuban force was reportedly heading towards Tombôco, some 420 kilometres due west of Maquela. A small but strategically important town due to it providing access to San Antonio do Zaire, the town in which Peter McAleese was stationed, Callan decided to leave straightaway to confront the enemy leaving his RSM 'Sammy' Copeland in charge. A particularly violent character, Copeland informed his own killer group that he was organising an ambush for that evening and that the men should prepare to be transported to Quibocolo from where they would advance on foot towards Damba.[95] In the meantime, a separate group was ordered to follow Copeland to Quibocolo a short time later while the non-combatants returned to their quarters at the base camp in Maquela. As the second group made its way through a checkpoint at Maquela, the Land Rover in which Chris Dempster, Tony Boddy and Barry Freeman were travelling came under a hail of fire. None of the vehicle's occupants being hurt, they realised that there were being shot at by the non-combatants who had mistaken them for Cubans.

As with any crime when mass murder has been committed and the perpetrators of that crime have attempted to absolve themselves from blame, the events taking place after the friendly-fire incident may vary in accordance with who provided the descriptions. Nevertheless, it is possible to provide a version that is generally accepted as being closest to the truth.

Around 2 a.m. in the morning of 2 February, two trucks were seen heading away from Maquela and making their way towards Zaire. After being pursued and stopped by FNLA soldiers under orders from Callan, when questioned the 23 men explained that Maquela had been attacked by Cubans and that they were simply defending their positions. Taken back to Maquela that same morning, they were ordered to line up in front of Callan. He told them that they were worthless compared to those they had almost killed, that they had deserted their positions by making a run for Zaire, and that in the British Army the penalty for desertion was death by hanging. The first of his own mercenary force killed by Callan that day was 22-year-old Philip Davies from Birmingham.[96] A former soldier, he owned up to having fired a rocket at the Land Rover and was shot three times in the head. The remaining men told to strip to their underpants, some like Kevin Marchant escaped punishment by volunteering for combat

T-34s, Lieutenant Abel Olivera Iraola was given the order to open fire using BM-21s.[93] After almost an hour of continuous firing and armoured vehicles plus infantry soldiers the 2nd Battalion and black troops of the MPLA's 9th Brigade ventured out to see the results of the barrage of fire. Unaware that all five of the advance party had survived the attack virtually unscathed, this joint force then came under sustained fire from machine guns, 66mm rockets and FNs. The mercenary force now waiting to be counter-attacked, no response came from an enemy that had retreated back to a safe distance. According to one source, the mercenary attack led to the deaths of 21 enemy soldiers,[94] while photographic evidence points to an abandoned or captured BM-21 being examined by the victors of this first skirmish between mercenaries and FAPLA forces.

Callan's battlefield strategy being to continue setting ambushes or sending out what he termed as 'killer groups' to hunt down enemy forces, on 29 January a contingent of 96 men recruited by Banks and Aspin arrived in Kinshasa where they were equipped with uniforms and Belgian FNs before being sent by coach to Maquela. The profile of the men that arrived at the FNLA's new HQ in Maquela on 30 and 31 January very much resembled that of those who had made up the first batch sent to Angola some two weeks beforehand. It included John Banks, Donald Taylor and the courier who had taken the money to London to pay for recruitment, and it also included the usual mix of ex-British paratroopers such as Cecil 'Satch' Fortuin. Others in the group were Vic Gawthorp and John Lockyear. Both suspected of belonging to MI6, their presence showed that the British government was taking a particular interest in what the British mercenaries were, or were not, doing. Out of the two only Lockyear was to return to the United Kingdom: Gawthorp died of a heart-attack on 3 February, the only non-violent death throughout the time FNLA mercenaries were in Angola.

Whereas Banks returned to the UK within the matter of a day or two, on 1 February the new recruits found themselves lined up before Callan. Explaining his 'killer' group strategy and telling them that the target was Cuban T-34 tanks, many complained duties. The remaining 11 men ordered aboard a Dodge troop carrier by Copeland, a Portuguese mercenary named Uzio drove the men out of Maquela followed by a Land Rover carrying four mercenaries and a second carrying a Portuguese-manned SG-43 Goryunov machine gun. Around three miles outside of Maquela the Dodge truck pulled up and off-loaded its cargo on to the road. Covered by the SG-43, the men were given one last chance at life and were told to run across a gully. While some refused to run and awaited their fate, the largest group that had managed to put 30 metres between themselves and their executioners were cut down by Copeland who was firing an Uzi machine gun. As the slaughter continued, Copeland, Boddy and Freeman made their way down into the valley where 8 of the mercenaries lay grievously wounded and began to administer fatal head shots.[97] All of those killed by Callan's forces had been in Angola for only a matter of 2-3 days and all were left unburied.

The murder of 12 men at Maquela did nothing to stop a two-month-long killing spree that also included the death of hundreds of black recruits at the hands of Callan, Copeland and Christodoulou and which was to continue until 15 February 1976.

Despite the gloom caused by the massacre of unarmed men, Callan's focus rapidly returned to the question of mounting another attack on the 'Cuban column' which, according to reports, had not moved from its position on the road to Damba. Another ambush was organised, and later on 2 February a column containing vehicles and some 25-30 mercenaries made its way from its base camp to Quibocolo in order to prepare for a tank-destruction mission. The trip to Quibocolo was not without incident: one of the Land Rovers hit a mine leaving three dead and others injured.[98] Having then returned to Maquela so that the injured could be treated, on 2-3 February, armed with M76 grenade launcher and grenades, and heavier weapons,[99] the column once again headed for Quibocolo. After reaching a small village and staying overnight,[100] on 3/4 February columns led by Callan and Copeland respectively made their way to Cuban/FAPLA positions that had been identified using aerial reconnaissance.[101] Callan ordering his column to mount a frontal attack, almost immediately it was ambushed by a force using powerful T-34 tanks. Though suffering some injuries (Ryan and Wilbor), the efforts of the mercenary force using 66mm rocket launchers destroyed four tanks and left over 200 enemy dead.[102] A further attack launched by Callan soon after saw Callan's killer group set up another ambush on the road to Damba.[103] This time involving 12 Cuban tanks, a number of BRDM-2 armoured cars, BM-21s, and 1,600 Cuban and Angolan troops, the Cuban convoy was led by Major Victor Correia Fernandes and a Russian advisor known as 'General Yuri'.[104]

The forces representing the MPLA allegedly included as many as 15 'Russians'.[105] The final battle, and what turned out to be Callan's last, was a particularly bloody affair and, once more, there appears to be confusion over exactly what happened. Though it certainly involved shelling from Cuban tanks accompanied by rifle fire, the deaths of the mercenaries and Cubans that ensued may have been caused by Callan firing a rocket launcher and blowing up a FAPLA ammunition truck.[106] In this version of events seconded by Marchant,[107] Callan, McKenzie, McIntyre and another unidentified British soldier were wounded, the latter dying soon after.[108] Another casualty was Tony Boddy though it is still not clear if he was killed by one of his own men.

The End of Mercenary Operations for the FNLA

As Callan and McKenzie sought shelter in a farmer's hut and awaited a rescue that would never come, reports of the Maquela Massacre and other atrocities committed on Callan's orders had reached Roberto. This resulted in Roberto, McAleese, Hall, Wainhouse and Tom Oates flying from Kinshasa to Maquela on 7 February. Having disarmed a group of mercenaries including Christodoulou and Copeland that had come to greet the plane with force, McAleese and Oates travelled to the scene of the massacre before reporting back to Roberto. Armed with photographic evidence that an atrocity had been committed, a court martial was hastily convened with Hall presiding over proceedings. In all seven witnesses testified against Christodoulou and Copeland. 'Shotgun' Charlie was found not guilty as he was not at Maquela when the massacre took place, but with Copeland being the main executioner he was sentenced to death by firing squad.

With McAleese promoted from Captain to Colonel after the hearings, and consequently becoming the FNLA's new field commander, thoughts very quickly turned back to the war taking place just a few kilometres from where Mick Wainhouse had finished off Copeland with three shots to the head. The Cuban/FAPLA troops were closing in on the São Salvador pocket using a classic Soviet Pincer strike on the two roads that took them east from Tombôco and south from Damba, but McAleese was faced with having to mount the defence of the area with depleted forces. Indeed, a good number of experienced mercenary fighters decided to leave Angola and make their way towards the safety of Kinshasa.

By the time McAleese's diminished force had pulled back to São Salvador to plan a counter-offensive, 'Brummy' Barker had been arrested by MPLA forces in San Antonio do Zaire and the British press had published a story on the Maquela Massacre. In turn, the US State Department immediately sought to distance itself from any implication in the events, which activist supporters of the MPLA in the United States gladly exploited as another reason to denounce the CIA's clandestine involvement in an African conflict.[109] Inevitably, the US Congress also stepped up efforts to limit what the CIA could and could not do in the name of the American people through the Tunney Amendment of 19 December 1975 to the proposed US Arms Export Control Act (1976). The CIA nonetheless finding funds elsewhere and being able to continue to supply weapons to the FNLA – five more flights from Washington and France to Kinshasa between 19 December 1975 and 29 January 1976[110] – the signing of the amendment on 9 February 1976 signalled the beginning of the end of Operation IA/FEATURE. Even the CIA, as Stockwell points out, made arms shipments: 22 flights left Kinshasa for an air strip in Gago Coutinho in eastern Angola delivering 145,900 pounds of arms and ammunition.[111] The FNLA's forces reduced to virtually nothing after Zairian withdrawal in mid-January, most of this weaponry was destined for UNITA forces. However, Savimbi having pulled back to Huambo and Porto Silva in the face of reportedly increased Soviet participation,[112] the writing was on the wall for a communist domination of Angola. There was to be, nevertheless, one final throw of the dice to bring support to the FNLA.

Though it was reported that anywhere between 600 and 4,000 mercenaries had been recruited to fight for the FNLA and UNITA, the reality is that the figure is likely to be closer to the lower estimate than the higher one: most Portuguese mercenaries were already in Angola; fewer than 100 and maybe even fewer than 50 French mercenaries fought in Cabinda for the FNLA and

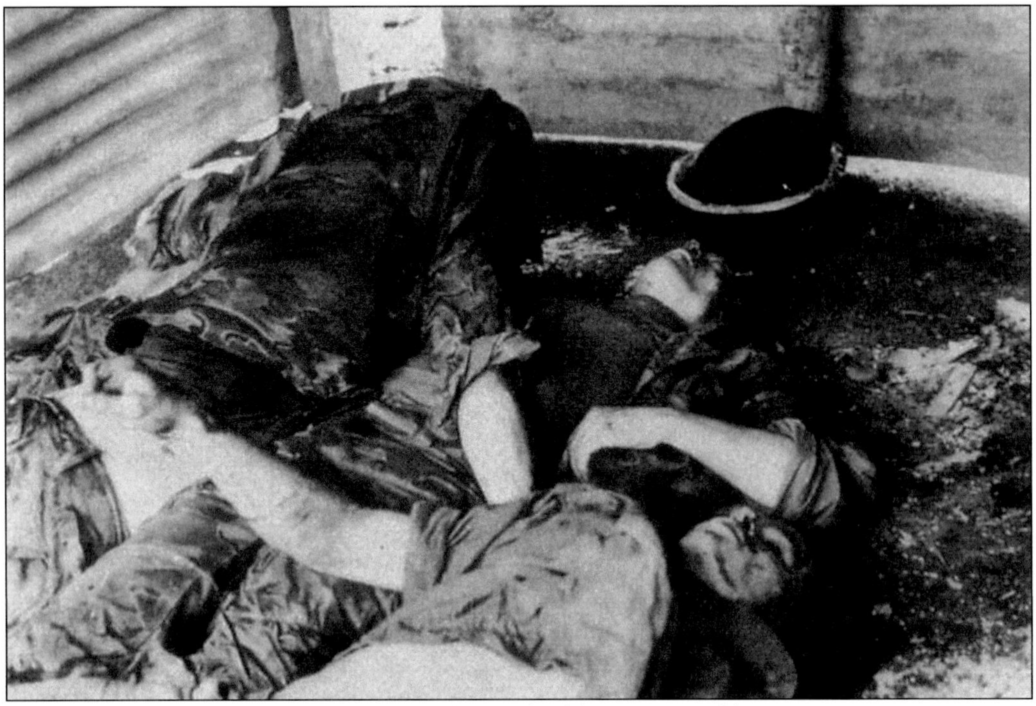

The bodies of dead mercenaries are piled up for the benefit of the Communist-bloc press.

The bodies of Canada Newby and two unidentified mercenaries bear the scars of recent battle with Cuban/FAPLA forces. One of those killed on 14 February 1976 was George Bacon III; he had been in Angola for just over one week.

for Savimbi's UNITA, and as far as it is known only around 120 mercenaries recruited by John Banks ever made it to Angola. A flight carrying 115 British mercenaries due to arrive in Kinshasa on or around 6 February was cancelled;[113] and by 16 February Mobutu had decreed new measures to stop mercenaries bound for Angola transiting through Kinshasa.[114]

In late 1975, we will remind ourselves, a former soldier named David Bufkin claimed to be the CIA's official mercenary recruiter for its operations in Angola, and to recruit what he bragged at the bar in the Kinshasa Intercontinental would be as many as 2,000 men,[115] Bufkin advertised in local Californian newspapers. Concurrently, there were two other organisations claiming to represent the CIA. Of the very few who replied to Bufkin's advertisement was Tom Oates who, along with Bufkin departed for Kinshasa on 26 January 1976. They then made contact with Roberto's secretary, Feliz Garcia Vimasiana. Bufkin was given $4,000 by the FNLA to fly back to the United States to recruit more Americans, and he returned to Kinshasa on 7 February with the grand total of six men: Lobo del Sol, Gustavo Grillo, Gary Acker, Daniel Gearhart and 29-year-old George Bacon III. Both Gearhart and Bacon using *Soldier of Fortune* magazine as a means to either advertise their services or to volunteer to fight for the FNLA, Bacon was a particularly experienced soldier in that he had served as a MACV-SOG operator in the Vietnam War before returning to southeast Asia as a CIA field officer in Laos.[116] Working alongside local anti-communist forces against the Pathet Lao, his actions saw him awarded the CIA's Intelligence Star.[117]

Bufkin and McAleese flying to São Salvador then Maquela on 7 February, they had time to survey the terrain and to realise that the ever-decreasing size of the FNLA was no match for the armoured column of around 70 fighting vehicles and the 2,000 Cuban/FAPLA troops making their way northwards through territory previously held by Roberto's men. Nonetheless, it was decided that an attempt would be made to defend São Salvador from forces also making their way eastwards from Tombôco. On 11 February, then, the remaining FNLA force of about 45 men including Portuguese mercenaries set out in three group with the intention of observing Cuban/FAPLA movement around Maquela. Two groups subsequently left for Cuimba on 14 February with similar intentions. While one of the Land Rovers in which they were travelling broke down and could not continue, the group comprising Christodoulou, Grillo, Gearhart, John Nammock and Andy Holland moved ahead in a single vehicle. Just before arriving in Cuimba, the Land Rover suddenly came under attack from a FAPLA vehicle parked a short distance up the road. Christodoulou was killed instantly as was Holland, Grillo and Nammock were injured, and though Grillo offered some resistance, it only took him a short time to realise that he was outgunned and that he would have to surrender.

South African forces withdraw from Angola at the end of March 1976.

While the survivors of this attack ended up in front of Angolan judges in Luanda some four months later, a group led by 'Canada' Newby hoped to attack the enemy convoy around Maquela. Unaware that those in Christodoulou's group were either dead, injured and/or captured, the plan was to retreat to São Salvador once the raid had been made and blowing up the bridge at Cuimba to deter the Cuban/FAPLA force from following. Newby's group made up of 12 men travelling in three Land Rovers,[118] it also encountered enemy forces on the road to Cuimba. In less than a minute, Bacon, Dimmock, Cashmore, Dickens and Newby were dead.

The End of Operation IA/FEATURE

No more proof was needed that the remaining 30 or so mercenaries were heavily outnumbered was needed after this last deadly encounter. Reconnaissance had shown that MPLA forces were just outside of São Salvador, that FNLA troops were throwing down their weapons in droves and heading back to Zaire, and that more mercenaries would be killed or captured they remained in the area. The last of the mercenaries still alive and/or not in the hands of Angolan authorities left Angola on 17 February 1976. It was a disaster for Roberto who would see his birthplace capitulate and who would see an end to plans to replace Neto as president and, in northern Angola at least, mercenary withdrawal signalled the end of Operation IA/FEATURE.

Further afield, diplomatic correspondence also seems to echo the death knell for any continued attempt to unseat the MPLA from its position in Luanda. France had indicated that it was on the point of recognising the MPLA as the government of Angola in order to protect its own interests in French-speaking Africa,[119] and Mobutu appeared to be holding talks with MPLA leaders that would bring about a ceasefire and the withdrawal of the last Zairian troops from Angolan soil. Any deal included the repatriation of the 6,000 Katanganese Gendarmes still supporting Neto's forces.[120] At an economic level, too, the context was changing rapidly. Even though the Department of State still maintained that UNITA could hold out for some time and was still planning to send arms shipments to Savimbi through Kinshasa as late as 20 February,[121] just a day later the *Washington Post* reported that Gulf Oil was seeking to carry out direct negotiations with the MPLA in order to resume its operations in Cabinda.[122] The State Department authorising this type of economic activity to go ahead, it also authorised Boeing to deliver two 737s to Neto's government. Boeing's technicians then travelled to Angola to install radar systems in Angolan airports.[123] Lastly, in moves of a military/economic nature, on 14 March it was reported that South Africa had announced that it would restrict any military activity to protecting its infrastructural interests around the Cunene hydroelectric project.[124] The MPLA guaranteeing that its forces would not attack the project, on 25 March South Africa then announced that it was to withdraw its remaining 3-4,000 combat troops. Having also obtained assurances surrounding the integrity of the border between Angola and South West Africa, this withdrawal was completed on 27 March.

As for UNITA, though the CIA did continue to send support despite the Tunney Amendment, Congressional pressure applied on CIA Director George Bush to phase out operations meant that Savimbi's forces were pushed back to the rear fringes of eastern Angolan territory once firmly in their hands. What help UNITA was receiving was being attacked by MPLA forces – a MiG-21 attack using 240mm S-24 heavy unguided rockets to destroy an Air Zaire Fokker F.27 at Gago Coutinho, and to attack the airport at Ninda near the border with Zambia in late March – Daniel Chipenda's forces were also breaking up. Indeed, while just under 3,000 remained with Chipenda, around 700 had now switched

The Luanda Trial took place from 11-19 June 1976.

allegiance and had joined MPLA forces, and another 3,000 had crossed the border into South West Africa where they were under the protection of South African forces.[125] Finally, with Cuba and the Soviet Union aid now brought to a total value of some $400 million as flight and ships brought in more supplies and troops, the CIA began to make payoffs to different parties involved in Operation IA/FEATURE. Colonel Santos Castro was given $243,000 on 25 February; $2 million was given to UNITA; Roberto received over $800,000; and of what remained of the $31.7 million budget for the operation as a whole, Mobutu was paid around $2 million. Some $600,000 of this being compensation for the Air Zaire Fokker F.27 destroyed by the MiG-21, Mobutu pocketed the remaining $1.4 intended for Angolans displaced by fighting.[126] Angola admitted as a member of the United Nations on 1 December 1976, three months earlier Neto expressed interest in establishing relations with the United States. Formal US recognition of Angola would not take place until May 1993.

The Luanda Trial

Whereas nearly 30 British mercenaries recruited by John Banks as well as David Bufkin returned to the United Kingdom or the United States in February 1976, 13 of the British and US citizens who left their home nations with hopes of fighting communism or simply earning a living were to face trial in Luanda from 11-19 June 1976. Captured by the MPLA around Damba and San Antonio do Zaire, the trial of these mercenaries followed indictment by the People's Revolutionary Court of Angola on 26 May 1976. On 5 June 1976, Luis de Almeida, the Director of Information and Security of Angola announced that the men were guilty of all the crimes with which they were charged, and the only role of the court in Luanda was to decide how the mercenaries should be punished. On 7 June, an exhibition was held in Luanda displaying some of the equipment used by the mercenaries as well as captured US currency, and on 9 June thousands of Angolans marched through Luanda holding placards that demanded the death penalty for those about to be judged. The trial being held in Luanda's Chamber of Commerce Building, the trial itself was conducted in Portuguese with simultaneous translation provided in English, Spanish, French and Russian mainly for the benefit of the 100 or so foreign journalists gathered in the upper balcony of the building. The court comprising five judges, its president was the Attorney General of Angola, Ernesto Teixeira da Silva, another was the Director of Angolan Television (a qualified judge in his own right), while the three remaining members were officers of the FAPLA and a representative of Angola's National Council of Women. The prosecution's final arguments presented on 17 June, Procurator Manuel Rui Alves Monteiro called on the court to sentence the mercenaries to death as a warning to other mercenaries tempted to fight in southern Africa.[127] Though US defence lawyers argued that the mercenaries should be considered as prisoners of war and, as such, should not be punished; and although British lawyers argued that the blame should be on the US and UK governments for allowing their recruitment, on 28 June the court in Angola announced its verdict.

FULL LIST OF CHARGES AND SENTENCES

Costas Georgiou – Death sentence

- Murder of a civilian in São Salvador on 7 January 1976
- Murder of an FNLA soldier in São Salvador
- Suspected murder of five civilians
- Ordering the suspected murder of two FNLA soldiers who appeared on parade without boots
- Ordering the killing of two FNLA soldiers in Quibocolo. They had appeared on parade without their uniforms
- Robbing an FNLA soldier of his watch and money then ordering him to be killed
- Murder of a British mercenary in Maquela
- Ordering the execution of 13 British mercenaries
- Torture and murder of an MPLA messenger.

Costas Georgiou was convicted of the murders of civilians, FAPLA soldiers and other mercenaries. He was executed by firing squad on 10 July 1976.

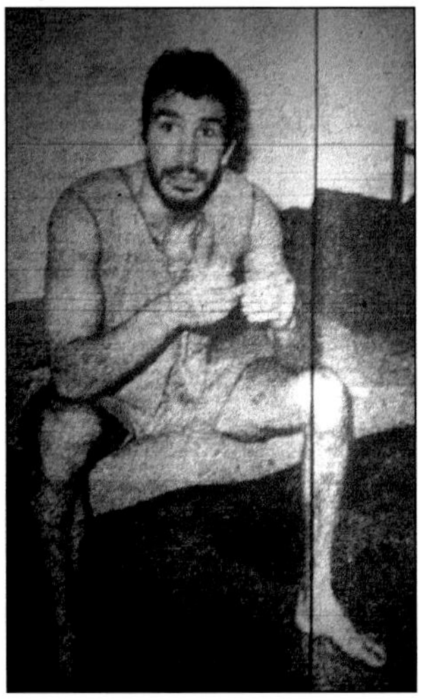

Georgiou seen seated in his prison cell awaiting execution.

Andrew Gordon McKenzie – Death Sentence

- Member of Georgiou's "killer" group"
- Armed action against FAPLA
- Planting of minefields
- Destruction, by the use of explosives, of bridges, buildings and military and civilian equipment and property
- Maltreatment, insults and harassment of civilian population
- Violation of homes and kidnapping of civilians, and their use as hostages
- Stealing of property
- Murder of other mercenaries.

Andrew McKenzie was convicted of taking an active part in the killing of British mercenaries and beating local civilians. McKenzie was executed by firing squad on 10 July 1976.

Derek John Barker – Death Sentence

- Gave military training to FNLA troops
- Commander of the FNLA's San Antonio garrison that oppressed, coerced and humiliated the local civilian population
- The planning of military operations including the planting of mines and the destruction of bridges.

Derek John 'Brummie' Barker was the commander of the FNLA military garrison at San Antonio do Zaire. Barker was sentenced to death and executed by firing squad on 10 July 1976.

Daniel Gearhart – Death Sentence

- Offered himself as a mercenary, placing an advert in the *Soldier of Fortune* magazine
- Commanded a combat section, and gave military training to FNLA troops
- Participated in actions against FAPLA
- Participated in the defence of São Salvador, setting mines and traps.

The death sentence is passed on McKenzie (in wheelchair), Georgiou (seated behind McKenzie), Gearhart (seated nearest Georgiou) and Barker. The fifth mercenary appears to be Grillo.

Michael Douglas Wiseman – 30 years imprisonment

- Member of a "Killer Group"
- Participated in armed actions against FAPLA. In particular, armed action at Damba and Quibocolo on 1 and 3 February in which FAPLA soldiers were injured and killed
- Took part in the plantation of minefields, and the destruction of bridges, buildings and civilian property.

Kevin John Marchant – 30 years imprisonment

- Member of a "Killer Group"
- Participated in armed actions against FAPLA. In particular, armed action at Damba and Quibocolo on 1 and 3 February in which FAPLA soldiers were injured and killed
- Took part in the plantation of minefields, and the destruction of bridges, buildings and civilian property
- Illegally occupied the property of peasant farmers.

Kevin Marchant was convicted of being a member of one of Georgiou's 'Killer Groups' and with killing FAPLA soldiers on 1 and 3 February 1976. Marchant was sentenced to 30 years imprisonment.

Gustavo Marcelo Grillo – 30 years imprisonment

- Participating in actions against FAPLA
- Organised security positions at São Salvador
- Commanded a combat unit composed of Americans, British and FNLA soldiers
- Provided training to FNLA soldiers
- Took part in actions against FAPLA on 13 February 1976.

Gustavo Grillo was convicted of participating in armed actions against FAPLA forces. He was sentenced to 30 years imprisonment.

Gustavo Grillo gives evidence during the Luanda Trial. An American of Argentine origin, Grillo was a veteran of the Vietnam War.

John Lawlor – 24 years imprisonment

- Participating in actions against FAPLA. In particular, armed action at Damba and Quibocolo on 1 and 3 February in which FAPLA soldiers were injured and killed
- Took part in the plantation of minefields, and the destruction of bridges, buildings and civilian property
- Illegally occupied the property of peasant farmers.

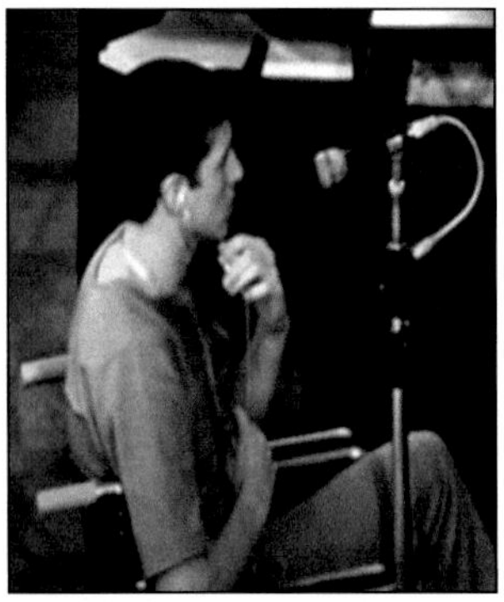

John Lawlor was convicted of participating in armed actions against FAPLA forces. He was sentenced to 24 years imprisonment.

Colin Clifford Evans – 24 years imprisonment

- Member of a "Killer Group"
- Participated in armed actions against FAPLA. In particular, armed action at Damba and Quibocolo on 1 and 3 February in which FAPLA soldiers were injured and killed
- Took part in the plantation of minefields, and the destruction of bridges, buildings and civilian property
- Illegally occupied the property of peasant farmers.

Cecil Martin Fortuin – 24 years imprisonment

- Member of a "Killer Group"
- Participated in armed actions against FAPLA. In particular, armed action at Damba and Quibocolo on 1 and 3 February in which FAPLA soldiers were injured and killed
- Took part in the plantation of minefields, and the destruction of bridges, buildings and civilian property
- Illegally occupied the property of peasant farmers.

John Nammock – 16 years imprisonment

- Participation in actions against FAPLA
- Took part in patrols as radio operator and took part in action against FAPLA on 13 February 1976.

John Nammock was convicted of participating in armed actions against FAPLA forces. He was sentenced to 16 years imprisonment.

Gary Martin Acker – 16 years imprisonment

- Collaborated in the recruitment of mercenaries
- Participated in the mounting of security operations at São Salvador
- Gave military training to FNLA
- Participated in actions against FAPLA at Cuimba.

Malcolm McIntyre – 16 years imprisonment

- Member of a "Killer Group"
- Participated in armed actions against FAPLA. In particular, armed action at Damba and Quibocolo on 1 and 3 February in which FAPLA soldiers were injured and killed
- Took part in the plantation of minefields, and the destruction of bridges, buildings and civilian property
- Illegally occupied the property of peasant farmers.

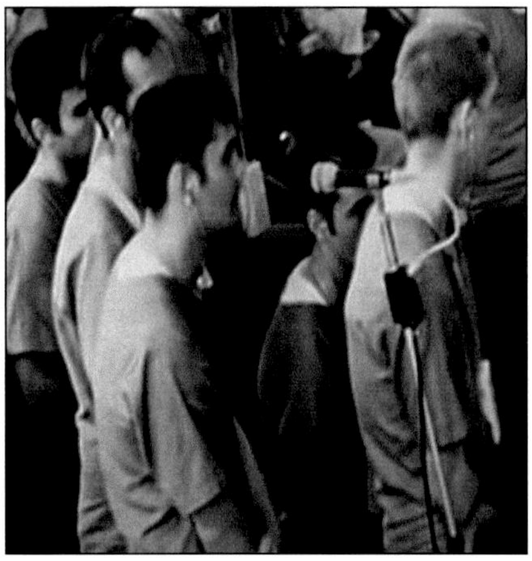

Malcolm McIntyre was also charged with being a member of the group that killed FAPLA soldiers on 1 and 3 February 1976. McIntyre was sentenced to 16 years imprisonment.

Despite many believing that the death sentences would be commuted to prison sentences, and despite appeals for clemency from President Ford, Queen Elisabeth, and British Prime Minister Harold Wilson, on 9 July 1976 Agostinho Neto confirmed that the executions would go ahead the following day. Explaining that the law was being applied not solely in the name of Angola but also to the "benefit of the brother peoples of Namibia and Zimbabwe", Neto stated that the sentence was for all the peoples of the world against whom imperialism is already preparing new mercenary aggressions".[128] The executions themselves took place at Grefanil military base around 20 miles outside of Luanda on 10 July 1976. As for the those sentenced to prison, both Grillo and Acker were released on 15 November 1982 after negotiations with the US government, and the remaining Britons were released in February 1984.

Concluding Remarks

After the success of US clandestine operations involving mercenaries in the Democratic Republic of the Congo, the CIA no doubt believed that mounting and funding similar operations in Angola would be a means of controlling the spread of what it perceived as another communist threat in Central Africa. The United States had installed Mobutu as president of the DRC and had supported him financially and militarily so as to ward off any dangers, so if changing or influencing the history of one country could be achieved at a relatively minimal cost without too much knowledge of CIA participation there was no reason why it could not be done again.

FACING THE FIRING SQUAD

THESE are the 10 British mercenaries soon to go on trial in Angola . . . and face the threat of death by firing squad.

It is the price they could pay for their ill-fated part in the Angolan War.

And as they wait for their trial—due to begin on June 8—the anguish of their families grows.

For since they were arrested three months ago, the new Angolan leaders have refused to let the men send messages home.

British mercenaries in Angola war trial

By JOHN HILL

The Foreign Office in London said: "We have been trying to get details from the Angolan authorities. But, so far, they have not responded."

Fainted

But, last night, one mother was giving thanks because, at long last, she knew that her 20-year-old son, John Nammock, was at least alive.

Mrs Noreen Nammock, of Hazelwood Crescent, West London, said: "Through a mix-up over the spelling of his name, I had been unable to discover whether he was really still alive.

"Now, because of details about his date of birth and past from Angola, I know that he is there.

"I nearly fainted when I heard the news. For months I have been ringing every telephone number I can think of where there might be some clue about him.

"He is the elder of my two sons and comes from an army family.

"John is the adventurous kind, whose idea of life is to be parachuting out of planes.

"I have been taking tranquillisers to help me sleep at night.

"Now I feel 100 times better—even though I am so worried about what will happen to him."

Caution

The list of Britons to be tried — announced by Angola's Justice Minister Dr Diogenes Boavida — is still being treated with caution by another mercenary's mother.

Mrs Catherine Lawlor, of Broom Hill Road, Farnborough Hants, said of her son also called John:

"I am 99 per cent sure that he is being held by them but I dare not positively believe it yet.

Fear

"Then there is the fear of what happens next.

"John is a strong character: — you do not go through Royal Marine training without becoming self-sufficient.

"But I would dearly love to be able to go to Angola for the trial.

COLONEL CALLAN

COSTAS GEORGIOU

● **HE is foremost among the accused mercenaries, who knew him as "Colonel" Callan.**

Georgiou, aged 25, is said to have ordered the deaths of 14 of his men for refusing to fight.

He is also alleged to be responsible for the massacre of 160 African villagers. He was born in Cyprus, but his parents live in London.

Kevin Marchant

● **HE once served in the Royal Artillery. His wife, from whom he is separated, has said: "He never cared about the money—only the fighting. Marchant, aged 25, comes from Borehamwood, Herts.**

Michael Wileman

● **HIS mother, who has six children, lives in Peckham, London. Wileman, aged 19, was still in council care when he signed up with the mercenaries.**

John Barker

● *He was captured while trying to flee Angola by swimming across the River Zaire. Barker, aged 30, is believed to have lived in Farnborough Hants.*

Colin Evans

● **HE is a father of four, but separated from his wife. Evans, aged 28, is a former regular Army soldier. His father lives in Dewsbury, Yorks.**

Cecil Fortuin

● *HE was born in Capetown, but brought up in the Midlands. Fortine, aged 32, was left for dead after being injured in Angola during an enemy advance.*

Malcolm McIntyre

● **His real name is Malcolm Wright. He is aged 27, a father of two, separated from his wife and was unemployed before joining the mercenaries.**

John Nammock

● *HE is an ex-Parachute Regiment soldier who lived in West London. Nammock, aged 20, comes from a family with a long Army connection.*

Andrew McKenzie

● *HE is another ex-Parachute Regiment man and a friend of mercenary Michael Wileman. McKenzie, aged 26, left the paras after six years.*

John Lawlor

● **HE is a former Marine from Farnborough, Hants. Lawler, aged 21, once did a term of duty in Ulster. Was reported killed in Angola.**

News of the trial was reported in many UK newspapers.

The main differences between what took place in the DRC in the 1960s and what took place in Angola in 1975/1976 were that the United States never seemed convinced that it could stop the MPLA from taking power. Rather, it would appear that Operation IA/FEATURE was an exercise in damage limitation knowing full well that it could not match Cuban and Soviet support, so the US made a series of ultimately futile attempts to put up some form of existential resistance in order for Ford and Kissinger to demonstrate that they took the question of communist interference in Africa seriously and that newly independent nations could not be given up to communism without a fight.

A second point is that in contrast to operations in the Congo where well organised mercenary forces overcame a disorganised and mainly untrained anti-government forces, the FAPLA supported by the armies of Cuba and the know-how of the Soviet Union presented a different type of foe. A more professional enemy, it was never going to be seriously threatened by armies whose main priority was the defence of outlying borders and economic interests (South Africa), or by outnumbered forces of mercenaries from different countries whose main interest was financial. The MPLA establishing itself as the legitimate authority in November 1975, the use of mercenaries in Angola as an attacking, rather than a defensive force also removed the United States own legitimacy. Though it was unaware that Georgiou was a psychopath and could not predict what actions would take place in Maquela in February 1976, using mercenaries in Angola ultimately damaged the standing of the United States on the international stage, particularly in Africa where it was perceived as unsympathetic to the needs and desires of its peoples. These sentiments were summed up by the presiding judge at the Luanda Trial who, in condemning the lack of control exerted by the US and British governments in relation to mercenary recruitment, accused both nations of being part of a "criminal conspiracy".[129]

List of English-speaking Mercenaries and Recruiters

Surname	First Name or Initial	Age	Origin	Regiment / Corps	Other information
Acker	Gary	21	Sacramento, USA	US Marines	16 years prison
Aiken	Daniel		UK	SBS	
Aimann	Richard		West Germany		
Aitken	Kenneth				
Arnold	S.		UK		KIA
Aspin	Leslie		UK	Royal Air Force	Recruiter
Aves *	Paul		UK		WIA, 03/02/76
Bacon III	George	29	USA	Green Beret, CIA	KIA, 14/02/76
Bufkin	David		USA	Pilot	
Baldwin	Andrew		UK		
Banks	John	30	Camberley, UK	Parachute Regiment	Recruiter
Barker*	Derek, John «Brummie»	35	Birmingham, UK	Parachute Regiment	Death Penalty
Bayliss	Ray		Chippenham, UK	Royal Marines	
Belford	Donald		Leeds, UK	FNLA Recruiter	
Birtwhistle			Leicester, UK	Pilot	WIA
Black	Andrew	21	UK	Pilot	
Blackmore	Robin	23	Watford, UK	Parachute Regiment	Murdered at Maquela
Boddy*	Tony	39		Parachute Regiment	KIA, 05/02/76
Bottomly			UK		Returned UK 18/02/76
Brooks	William	23	Boreham Wood, UK	Civilian Driver	Murdered at Maquela
Bufkin	David		USA		
Butcher	Ray		Bournemouth,UK	Parachute Regiment	
Canes	Sidney		UK		
Canning	Vincent		Ealing, UK	Foreign Legion	
Carrol	P.T.		UK		
Carter	Sidney		UK		KIA
Cashmore	John		UK		KIA, 14/02/76
Cassidy			UK	Parachute Regiment	
Chambers	James		UK		
Christodoulou	Charles		UK	Parachute Regiment	KIA, 14/02/76
Coleman	Patrick		UK		
Copeland*	Raymond «Sammy»	29	UK	Parachute Regiment	Death Penalty (mercenary court)
Davies	Philip		Birmingham, UK		Murdered by Georgiou, 02/02/76 1
Deacon			UK		
Dempster*	Chris		UK	Royal Artillery	
Del Sol	Lobo	25	USA		

1 In another account, the name of the man killed by Callan is listed as David Wileman.

Surname	First Name or Initial	Age	Origin	Regiment / Corps	Other information
Dickens			UK	Parachute Regiment	KIA, 14/02/76
Dimmock	Malcolm		UK		KIA, 14/02/76
Elford	Lewis		UK		
Ellis	Allen		Leeds, UK		
Evans	Colin	28	UK		24 years prison
Feiry	John		UK		
Fortuin	Cecil, Martin «Satch»		UK / South Africa	Parachute Regiment	24 years prison
Freeman*	Barry		Manchester, UK		
Gawthorp	Brian		Cambridge, UK	Cook	
Gawthorp	Victor		Cambridge, UK	Suspected MI6	Died from heart attack, 03/02/76
Georgoiu	Costas «Colonel Callan»	25	UK	Parachute Regiment	Death penalty
Gearheart	Daniel	34	Maryland, USA		Death penalty
Geary	Terry		Romford, UK		
Griffiths*	Garnett, John «Stars»		UK		
Grillo	Gustavo	27	Argentina / USA		30 years prison
Grundy			UK		
Hammond	Paul		UK		
Hart	David		UK		
Hall	Mervyn 'Nick'	21	UK	Parachute Regiment	Recruiter and FNLA Major
Heaton	David	30	Plymouth, UK	Civilian driver	Murdered at Maquela
Henderson	Keith		Liverpool, UK		Returned to UK, 18/02/76
Hill			Rochdale, UK		WIA
Hillaney	Morgan		UK		
Holland	Andrew		UK	Parachute Regiment	KIA, 14/02/76
Hussey*	«Fuzz»		UK		KIA, 14/02/76
James			UK		
Jarman			UK		
Jenkinson	Roger		UK		
Johnson*	Michael		Chichester, UK	Royal Marines	KIA
Jones	F. «Geordie»		Tyneside, UK		WIA, 03/02/76
Jones	«Freddie»		Andover, UK		WIA, 07/02/76
Kay	John	27	Bradford, UK	Royal Dragoon Guards	Murdered at Maquela
Kelly	John «Spider»		UK		
Keray	Victor		UK		WIA
Kesterton	Tony		Windsor, UK		
Kildunne			Bury, UK		
Kovacz	Lazlo		Hungary		
Lawlor	John				24 years prison
Leach			UK		
Lockyear	John			Suspected MI6	

Surname	First Name or Initial	Age	Origin	Regiment / Corps	Other information
Lewis*	Bryan	19	Camberley, UK		
Lynch			UK		
Madison	Barry	29	London, UK	SAS	
Malloy	Terry		UK		Returned UK, 18/02/76
Malone	John		Glasgow, UK		
Marchant	Kevin	25	Borehamwood, UK	Parachute Regiment	30 years prison
Marczynski	James	24	Bradford, UK	Coldstream Guards	Murdered at Maquela
Maynard			Slough, UK		
McAleese*	Peter	33	Glasgow, UK	SAS	
McAleese #	Thomas		Glasgow, UK	Parachute Regiment	
McCandless*	Jamie		UK	SAS	Presumed KIA
McCartney	Andrew 'Jock'	52	Perth, UK	Civilian	Murdered at Maquela
McCulloch			UK		
McIntyre	Malcolm	26	Perth, UK	Parachute Regiment	16 years prison
McKay	Patrick		UK	Parachute Regiment	
McKenzie*	Andrew	24	UK	Parachute Regiment	Death penalty
McKeown	Michael		UK		
McPhearson*	Patrick		UK		
McPhearson*	Stuart		UK		
Mellstrom			UK		
Molyneaux	K.		UK		
Morris	Michael		UK		Returned from Kinshasa, 18/02/76
Morrison	Hugh		UK	Ex-Foreign Legion	Injured in road accident and taken back to Kinshasa, 30/01/76
Moss	Charles		UK		
Mott	Malcolm	19	UK	Civilian mechanic	Murdered at Maquela
Munday			Kettering, UK		Suspected KIA
Myers	Leslie		UK		Returned from Kinshasa, 18/02/76
Nammock	John		Ireland		16 years prison
Newby	Douglas «Canada»		Canada		KIA, 14/02/76
Newton			UK		
Nilbor	Barry		UK		WIA
Oates	Thomas		USA	Suspected CIA	Arrived 04/02/76
O'Brien	Dennis		Camberley, UK		WIA, 03/02/76
O'Shea			UK	Parachute Regiment	
Oates	Thomas		USA		unknown
Oram	Clifford	29	Yorkshire, UK	Parachute Regiment	Murdered at Maquela
Paden	David		UK	Parachute Regiment	

Surname	First Name or Initial	Age	Origin	Regiment / Corps	Other information
Patay	Laslo		Hungary		
Perrin	Frank			SBS	
Pullen	Max				Returned UK from Kinshasa, 18/02/76
Randall	Barry	23	Hemel Hempstead, UK	Parachute Regiment	Murdered at Maquela
Ranson			Braintree, UK		
Rennie*	Mick		Dulwich, London, UK	Parachute Regiment	Returned from Kinshasa, 18/02/76
Richmond	R.				
Risbridger	Max	20	Hove, UK	Foreign Legion	Possibly murdered at Maquela or KIA
Roden	Frank		Coventry, UK		
Rolls	Peter		UK		WIA
Ryan	Fred		Wakefield, UK		WIA, 05/02/76
Saunders	Dale, Richard		UK		Returned from Kinshasa, 18/02/76
Saunders	Douglas		UK		Returned from Kinshasa, 18/02/76
Salmon					
Scaley	Eugene		USA		Took refuge in US Embassy
Serivenis			Marlow, UK		KIA
Sharpley			UK	Parachute Regiment	
Shire	Tony		Wales, UK		
Slogget	Ben		UK	Parachute Regiment	
Smith	Brian	26	Warrington, UK	Royal Green Jackets	Murdered at Maquela
Smith	David	26	London, UK	Royal Green Jackets	
Souter			Glamorgan, UK		
Spence			UK		
Stanley	David		UK		
Talbot	A.		UK		
Taylor	Colin		UK	Recruiter	
Tilsey*	David «Bert»		UK		
Tomkins*	David				
«Uncle Dan»					
Wainhouse	Michael				
Ward	Andrew	20	Copthorne, UK		Murdered at Maquela
Webb	Harry	36	Leeds, UK	Civilian driver	Murdered at Maquela
Whirity	Kevin	30	UK	Parachute Regiment	
White	Terence		Farnborough, UK	Pilot	
White	Max		Luton, UK		
Wilbot or Wilbor	Barry		Rhodesia	SAS	WIA, 05/02/76
Wild	B.G.		South Africa		KIA
Wileman	Michael or David	19	London, UK		Murdered at Maquela

Surname	First Name or Initial	Age	Origin	Regiment / Corps	Other information
Wilson	Terence		Rhodesia	SAS	WIA
Wiseman	Michael				16 years prison
Wright	Michael F.J.		UK/Rhodesia	SAS	
Young	William			Parachute Regiment	Returned to UK, 18/02/76

* Denotes part of second advance party that left the UK on 18 January 1976.

# Denotes recruited for second advance party but did not travel.

Adapted from lists compiled by Peter McAleese, *No Mean Soldier*, and "UK mercenaries in Angola", FCO 45/1889, 1 January-31 December 1976.

Bibliography

Primary Sources (Mémoires)

Aspin, Leslie, with Aspinall, Trevor, *I, Kovaks* (London: Everest Books Limited, 1975).

Banks, John, *The Wages of War: The Life of a Modern Mercenary* (London: Leo Cooper, 1978).

Dempster, Chris, & Tomkins, Dave with Parry, Michael, *Fire Power* (London: Corgi Books, 1978).

McAleese, Peter, *No Mean Soldier* (London: Orion Books Ltd, 1993).

Spínola, Antonio de, *Portugal E O Future* (Peskor, 1974).

Stockwell, John, *In Search of Enemies* (London: Futura Publications Limited, 1979).

Primary Sources (Archival documents)

"40 Committee Decisions", Department of State, INR/IL Historical Files, Intelligence Committee Report File, 40 Committee, 22 January 1975.

"40 Committee Meeting", 5 June 1975. National Security Council, Ford Administration Intelligence Files, 40 Committee Meetings.

"40 Committee Meeting, 14 July 1975, National Security Council, Ford Administration Intelligence Files, 40 Committee Meetings.

"40 Committee Meeting", 8 August 1975. National Security Council, Ford Administration, Intelligence Files, 40 Committee Meetings.

"40 Committee Meeting, 14 November 1975", National Security Council, Ford Administration, Intelligence Files, 40 Committee Meetings.

"40 Committee Meeting", 21 November 1975, NSC, Ford Administration Files, Intelligence Files, 40 Committee Meetings.

"Africa", Washington, 20 June 1975. Library of Congress Manuscript Division, Kissinger Papers, Box CL 102, Geopolitical File, Angola Chronological File.

"Alleged Assassination Plots Involving Foreign Leaders", An Interim Report of the Select Committee to Study Governmental Operations with Respect to Intelligence Activities (Washington: US Government Printing Office, 1975).

"Amendment Law No.2048, 11 June 1951", as quoted in *John Marcum, The Angolan Revolution: Volume 1: The Anatomy of an Explosion (1950-1962)* (MIT Press: Cambridge, MASS and London, 1969).

"Angola", Washington, 11 June 1975. Library of Congress Manuscript Division, Kissinger Papers, Box CL 102, Geopolitical File, Angola Chronological File.

"Branaman Chronology", in "Mercenaries in Africa", Hearing before the Subcommittee on Investigations of the Committee on International Relations, House of Representatives, 94th Congress, Washington, 9 August 1976.

"Captain Ferreira Valencia's Report, 'A Abrilada 1961' (1977), AHM Division 1, Section 39, Box 1, Documents 1 and 3.

"Chronology, December 1974-February 1975", *Pakistan Horizon* (published by Pakistan Institute of International Affairs), Vol.28, No.1, First Quarter, 1975, pp.66-143.

Collelo Thomas (ed.), "Angola: a Country Study" Federal Research Division, Library of Congress, February 1989.

"Country Summary Prepared in the Bureau of Intelligence Research, Washington, 6 March 1967", Document 442, FRUS, 1964-1968, Vol. XXIV, Africa.

"Dini on Prospects of Congolese Economy", Vance, Kinshasa to Secretary of State, 2 July 1970, RG 59, Economic, Box 787, Department of State, NARA II.

"Hearings before the Subcommittee on Africa of the Committee on Foreign Affairs, House of Representatives", 96th Congress, 17-30 September 1980.

Lowenthal, Mark, M.,"Foreign Assistance in the Angolan Civil War: Chronology of Reported Events, 1975-1976", Congressional Research Service (CRS) Library of Congress, 8 June 1976.

"Memorandum of Conversation", Washington, 17 July 1975. Library of Congress, Manuscript Division, Kissinger Papers, Box CL 282, Memoranda of Conversations, Presidential File, 17 July 1975.

"Memorandum of Conversation", Washington, 25 July 1975. Library of Congress, Manuscript Division, Kissinger Papers, Box CL 102, Geopolitical File, Angola Chronological File.

"Memorandum from the Executive Secretary of the 40 Committee (Ratliff) to Director of Central Intelligence Colby", 28 July 1975. Natioanl Security Council, Ford Administration Intelligence Files, 40 Committee meetings.

"Memorandum of Conversation", Meeting with Congo (K) President Mobutu: Portugal and Angola (Part 3 of 5), Washington, 4 August 1970, NARA, RG 59, Central files, 1970-73, POL 17.

"Memorandum of Conversation", 19 November 1975, Kissinger Papers, Box CL 103, Geopolitical File, Angola Chronological File.

"*Military Facilities in the Azores: Agreement between Portugal and the United States*", 6 September 1951, American Foreign Policy 1950-1955, Basic Documents Volumes I and II, Department of State Publication 6446, General Foreign Policy Series 117, Washington, DC : U.S. Government Printing Office, 1957.

"Minutes of a National Security Council Meeting", Washington, 27 June 1975. Ford Library, National Security Advisor, NSC Meetings File, Box 2, NSC Meeting, 27 June 1975.

"Mobutu's Request for Material Support to Holden Roberto", Washington, 19 September 1974. Ford Library, National Security Adviser, Outside the System Chronological File, Box 1.

"National Security Council Meeting" Washington, 25 July 1960, Central Intelligence Agency Files, Job 79R00890A, Box 13, Folder 1, NSC Briefings, July 1960.

"Plan for Covert Action -Angola", Department of State, INR/IL Historical Files, Africa, Latin America, Inter-Agency Intelligence Committee Files, Angola-Washington.

"Private Meeting between UNITA President Savimbi and Zairian President Mobutu", 9 June 1975. Library of

Congress Manuscript Division, Kissinger Papers, Box CL 102, Geopolitical File, Angola Chronological File.
"Report Prepared by the Working Group on Angola", *Military Matériel Sent to Zaire Under the Angola Covert Paramilitary Program*, Washington, 20 February 1976, Kissinger Papers, Box CL 104.
"Report Prepared by the Working Group on Angola", Washington, 2 April 1976, Kissinger Papers, Box CL 104.
"Response to NSSM 224: United States Policy Toward Angola", Washington, 13 June 1975, Department of State, INR/IL Historical Files, Africa, Latin America, Inter-Agency Intelligence Committee Files, Angola, NSSM 224.
"The Robert Vesco Investigation", aka, "Hearings before the Permanent Subcommittee on Investigations of the Committee on Government Operations, United States Senate", 22 July, 17 September, and 7 October 1974.
"Short-Term Prospects for the Africain Nationalist Movements in Angola and Mozambique", Special National Intelligence Estimate, Number 71-64, 1 July, 1964.
"Soviet and Cuban Aid to the MPLA in Angola from March through December 1975", Interagency Intelligence Memorandum, 24 January 1976.
"Soviet and Cuban Intervention in The Angolan Civil War", Central Intelligence Agency, Directorate of Intelligence, March 1977.
"Soviet Military Policy in the Third World", National Intelligence Estimate, 21 October 1976.
"Telegram from the Embassy in Zaire to the Department of State", Kinshasa, 24 July 1975. National Archives, RG 59, Central Foreign Policy Files, P840178 – 1917.
"Telegram from Secretary of State Kissinger to the Embassy in France", 14 February 1976, National Archives, RG 59, Central Foreign Policy Files, P840086-1506.
"United States Policy Toward Angola", Washington, 26 May 1975. Ford Library, National Security Adviser, NSDMs and NSSMs, Box 2, NSSMs File, NSSM 224.
"USSR-Africa: Soviets Increasing Aid to African Liberation Fronts?", Washington, 11 August 1970. Department of State, INR/IL Historical files, Africa, Latin America, Inter-Agency Intelligence Committee Files, Angola-Washington.
"US-Zaire Relations", Washington, 12 August 1974. Library of Congress, Manuscript Division, Kissinger Papers, Box CL 257, Geopolitical File, Zaire, August 1974-June 1975.

Secondary Sources (Monographs)

Burchett, Wilfred & Roebuck, Derek, *The Whores of War: Mercenaries Today* (London: Penguin Books, 1977).
Dorril, Stephen, *MI6: Inside the Covert World of Her Majesty's Secret Intelligence Service* (London: Free Press, 2002).
Fontanellaz, A. & Cooper, T., *War of Intervention in Angola, Volume 1: Angolan and Cuban Forces at War, 1975-1976* (Warwick: Helion & Co., 2018)
Fontanellaz, A., *War of Intervention in Angola, Volume 2: Angolan and Cuban Forces at War, 1976-1983* (Warwick: Helion & Co., 2019)
Flintham, Victor, *Air Wars and Aircraft: A Detailed Record of Air Combat, 1945 to the Present* (London: Arms and Armour Press, 1989).
Franklin, Jane, *Cuba and the US Empire: A Chronological History* (New York: Monthly Review Press, 2016).
George, Edward, *The Cuban Intervention in Angola, 1965-1991: From Che Guevara to Cuito Cuanavale* (London & New York: Frank Cass, 2005).
Gleijeses, Piero, *Conflicting Missions: Havana, Washington and Africa, 1959-1976* (Chapel Hill and London: The University of North Carolina Press, 2002).
Guimaraes, Fernando Andresen, *The Origins of the Angolan Civil War: Intervention and Domestic Political Conflict* (London: Palgrave Macmillan, 2001).
Harsch, Ernest, and Thomas, Tony, *Angola: The Hidden History of Washington's War* (New York: Pathfinder Press, 1976).
Lamb, Christopher John, *Belief Systems and Decision Making in the Mayaguez Crisis* (Gainesville: University of Florida Press, 1989).
Loftus, John and Aarons, Mark, *The Secret War Against the Jews: How Western Espionage Betrayed the Jewish* People (New York: St Martin's Griffin,1994).
Marcum, John, *The Angolan Revolution, Volume II: Exile Politics and Guerrilla Warfare*, 1962-1976 (Michigan, USA: The MIT Press, 1978).
Murphy, Jack, "MACV – SOG Operator, CIA Para-Military Officer, Mercenary, and Genius", *Sofrep*, 24 May 2012.
Nzongola-Ntalaja, Georges, *The Congo from Leopold to Kabila: A People's History* (London: Zed Books, 2002).
Onimode, Bade, *A Political Economy of the African Crisis* (London: Zed Books, 1988).
Porter, Bruce D., *The USSR in Third World Conflicts: Soviet Arms and Diplomacy in Local Wars, 1945– 1980* (London: Cambridge University Press, 1984).
Renton, David, Seddon, David, and Zelig, Leo, *The Congo: Plunder and Resistance* (London: Zed Books, 2007).
Rookes, Stephen, *Ripe for Rebellion: Political and Military Insurgency 1946-1964* (Warwick: Helion & Co., 2020).
Rookes, Stephen, *For God and the CIA: Cuban Exile Operations in the Congo and Beyond, 1959-1967* (Warwick: Helion & Co., 2020).
Schraeder, Peter, J., *United States Foreign Policy Toward Africa: Incrementalism, Crisis, and Change* (New York: Cambridge University Press, 1994).
Thornton, John, "Mbanza Kongo/São Salvador: Kongo's Holy City", in David Anderson and Richard Rathbone (eds.), *Africa's Urban Past* (James Currey Ltd.: Oxford, 2000), p.73.
Weigert, Stephen, L., *Angola: A Modern Military History, 1961-2002* (London: Palgrave Macmillan, 2001).
Weiner, Tim, *Legacy of the Ashes: The History of the CIA* (New York: Anchor, 2008).

Secondary Sources (Academia)

(Author unknown), "*Military Balance*", *Institute of Strategic Studies* (London, 1967), p.26.
Calvão, A., "De Conacry ao MDLP", dossier secreto, *Intervenção*, Lisbon, 1976.
Gleijeses, Piero, "Cuba's First Venture in Africa: Algeria, 1961-1965, *Journal of Latin American Studies*, 1996, p.160.
Heimer, Franz-Wilhelm, " The Decolonization Conflict in Angola, 1974-76: An Essay in Political Sociology", *International Studies on Contemporary Africa Series*, Institut universitaire de hautes études internationales, 1979, pp.56-57.

Heywood, Linda M., "Slavery and its Transformation in the Kingdom of the Kongo, 1491-1800", *The Journal of African History*, Vol.50, No.1 (2009), pp.1-22.

Heywood, Linda M., "Angola and the Violent Years 1975-2008: Civilian Casualties", *Portuguese Studies Review*, Vol.19, Issue 1-2, January-July 2011, p.316.

Hoover, Mike J. "The Laws of War and the Angolan Trial of Mercenaries: Death to the Dogs of War", *Case Western Reserve Journal of International Law*, Volume 9, Issue 2, 1977.

Jackson, Steven F.,"China's Third World Policy: The Case of Angola and Mozambique, 1961-93", *The China Quarterly*, No.142, June 1995, p.397.

Lobato, Gisele, "The Strange Case of Brazilian Support to the FNLA in the Final Stage of Angolan Decolonization", *afriche e oriente*, Number 3, 2017, p.34.

Lockwood, George, "Report on the Trial of Mercenaries", Luanda, Angola – June, 1976.

Marcum, John, "Lessons of Angola", *Foreign Affairs*, 54, April 1976, pp.407-425.

Noer, Thomas J., "International Credibility and Political Survival: The Ford Administration's Intervention in Angola", *Presidential Studies Quarterly*, Fall, 1993, Vol.23, No.4, pp.771-785.

Osuna, José Javier Olivas, "The Deep Roots of the Carnation Revolution: 150 years of military interventionism in Portugal", *Portuguese Journal of Social Science*, 13 (2), pp.215-231.

Reis, Bruno Cardoso, "Portugal and the UN: A Rogue State Resisting the Norm of Decolonisation", *Modern Humanities Research Association,* Vol.29, No.2, pp.251-276.

Shubin, Vladimir, "The USSR and Southern Africa during the Cold War", *Centro di Studi Storica e Politica su Africa e Medio Oriente*, Occasional Paper 1, November 2008, Bologna, p.4.

Stevens, Chistopher, "The Soviet Union and Angola", *African Affairs*, Vol.75, No.299, April 1976, p.144.

Valdes, Nelson, "Revolutionary Solidarity in Angola", in *Cuba in the World* (eds. Cole Blasier and Carmelo Mesa-Lago) (Pittsburgh: University of Pittsburgh Press, 1979), p.91.

Wheeler, Douglas L., "The Portuguese Army in Angola", *The Journal of Modern African Studies*, Vol.7, No.3, October 1969, pp.425-439.

Newspaper Articles (by date)

"Cuba Began Role in Zanzibar in '61: Havana's Part in Revolution Outlined in Washington – Guerrilla Course Cited", *New York Times*, 2 January 1964.

"Azores Agreement Means Increased US Backing of Colonial Wars", *American Committee on Africa*, 10 December 1971.

"Why We Protest Gulf Oil in Angola", *American Committee on Africa*, June, 1973.

Hersh, Seymour M., "Huge CIA Operation Reported in US Against Antiwar Forces, other Dissidents in Nixon Years", *New York Times*, 22 December 1974.

Binder, David, (Title unknown), *New York Times*, 13 December 1975.

Stern, Laurence, "The Angola Mercenary Caper", *Washington Post*, 9 January 1976.

Johnson, Thomas A., (Title unknown), *New York Times*, 11 February 1976.

Robin Wright, "Talkative Mercenary Claims CIA Tie", *The Washington Post*, 6 May 1977.

(Author unknown), "Victor Dreke Cruz: Cuba's history man still talks of revolution", *The Independent*, 17 April, 2011.

Digital Sources

"Charter of the United Nations, Chapter XI, Article 73-Declaration Regarding Non-Self-Governing Territories", <https://legal.un.org/repertory/art73.shtml>, accessed 23 July 2020.

"Country Comparison: life expectancy at birth", available at <https://www.cia.gov/library/publications/the-world-factbook/fields/355rank.html#AO>, accessed 21 April 2020.

Homer, Jack A., "Angola: Repression and Revolt in Portuguese Africa", *African Committee on Africa*, 1960, p.7, <http://kora.matrix.msu.edu/files/50/304/32-130-1906-84-ACOA_Angola_Homer_Jack_opt.pdf>, accessed 27 July 2020.

"Inter-Allied Meeting", *United Nations Documents, 1941-1945*, p.9, <https://histdoc.net/pdf/United_Nations_docs_pp.9-11.pdf>, accessed 23 July 2020.

"Oil Embargo, 1973-1974", US Department of State, Office of the Historian, <https://history.state.gov/milestones/1969-1976/oil-embargo>, accessed 2 December 2020.

"People and Society of Angola", <https://www.cia.gov/library/publications/the-world-factbook/geos/ao.html>, accessed 21 April 2020.

"Portugal Inflation Rate, 1960-2020", <https://www.macrotrends.net/countries/PRT/portugal/inflation-rate-cpi>, accessed 12 February 2021.

"Speech of Dr. Fidel Castro at the UN General Assembly, September 1960", <http://www1.lanic.utexas.edu/project/castro/db/1960/19600926.html>, accessed 23 June 2018.

"'The Atlantic Charter': Declaration of Principles issued by the President of the United States and the Prime Minister of the United Kingdom", 14 August 1941, <https://www.nato.int/cps/en/>, accessed 23 July 2020.

"The Languages of Angola", <https://www.goethe.de/prj/lat/en/ide/spr.html>, accessed 21 April 2020.

Doctoral Thesis

Bechtolsheimer, G., *Breakfast with Mobutu: Congo, the United States and the Cold War, 1964-1981,* PhD Thesis, The London School of Economics and Political Science, 2012, available at http://etheses.lse.ac.uk/403/.

Notes

Chapter 1

1 Linda M. Heywood, "Slavery and its Transformation in the Kingdom of the Kongo, 1491-1800", *The Journal of African History*, Vol.50, No.1 (2009), pp.1-22.

2 John Thornton, "Mbanza Kongo/São Salvador: Kongo's Holy City", in David Anderson and Richard Rathbone (eds.), *Africa's Urban Past* (James Currey Ltd.: Oxford, 2000), p.73.

3 "Amendment Law No.2048, 11 June 1951", as quoted in *John Marcum, The Angolan Revolution: Volume 1: The Anatomy of an Explosion (1950-1962)* (MIT Press: Cambridge, MASS and London, 1969), p.5.

4 Jack A. Homer, "Angola: Repression and Revolt in Portuguese Africa", *African Committee on Africa*, 1960, p.7, <http://kora.matrix.msu.edu/files/50/304/32-130-1906-84-ACOA_Angola_Homer_Jack_opt.pdf>, accessed 27 July 2020

5 Homer, "Angola: Repression and Revolt in Portuguese Africa", p.7 in *John Marcum, The Angolan Revolution: Volume 1: The Anatomy of an Explosion (1950-1962)* (MIT Press: Cambridge, MASS and London, 1969), p.5.

6 Marcum, *The Angolan Revolution: Volume 1: The Anatomy of an Explosion (1950-1962)*, p.5.

7 "The Languages of Angola", <https://www.goethe.de/prj/lat/en/ide/spr.html>, accessed 21 April 2020.

8 "People and Society of Angola", <https://www.cia.gov/library/publications/the-world-factbook/geos/ao.html>, accessed 21 April 2020.

9 "Country Comparison: life expectancy at birth", <https://www.cia.gov/library/publications/the-world-factbook/fields/355rank.html#AO>, accessed 21 April 2020.

Chapter 2

1 "Inter-Allied Meeting", *United Nations Documents, 1941-1945*, p.9, <https://histdoc.net/pdf/United_Nations_docs_pp.9-11.pdf>, accessed 23 July 2020.

2 "'The Atlantic Charter': Declaration of Principles issued by the President of the United States and the Prime Minister of the United Kingdom", 14 August 1941, <https://www.nato.int/cps/en/,>, accessed 23 July 2020.

3 "Charter of the United Nations, Chapter XI, Article 73- Declaration Regarding Non-Self-Governing Territories", <https://legal.un.org/repertory/art73.shtml>, accessed 23 July 2020.

4 Bruno Cardoso Reis, "Portugal and the UN: A Rogue State Resisting the Norm of Decolonisation", *Modern Humanities Research Association*, Vol.29, No.2, pp.251-276.

5 Another of the MPLA's founding members was Viriato da Cruz. Like Andrade, Da Cruz was a prominent poet in that period.

6 Linda M. Heywood, "Angola and the Violent Years 1975-2008: Civilian Casualties", *Portuguese Studies Review*, Vol.19, Issue 1-2, January-July 2011, p.316.

7 Edward George, *The Cuban Intervention in Angola, 1965-1991: From Che Guevara to Cuito Cuanavale* (London & New York: Frank Cass, 2005), p.9.

8 Fernando Andresen Guimaraes, *The Origins of the Angolan Civil War: Intervention and Domestic Political Conflict* (London: Palgrave Macmillan, 2001), p.53.

9 "Angola: a Country Study" (Edited by Thomas Collelo), Federal Research Division, Library of Congress, February 1989.

10 Steven F. Jackson, "China's Third World Policy: The Case of Angola and Mozambique, 1961-93", *The China Quarterly*, No.142, June 1995, p.397.

11 "Oil Embargo, 1973-1974", US Department of State, Office of the Historian, <https://history.state.gov/milestones/1969-1976/oil-embargo>, accessed 2 December 2020.

12 "Portugal Inflation Rate, 1960-2020", <https://www.macrotrends.net/countries/PRT/portugal/inflation-rate-cpi>, accessed 12 February 2021.

13 "Captain Ferreira Valencia's Report, 'A Abrilada 1961' (1977), AHM Division 1, Section 39, Box 1, Documents 1 and 3 in, José Javier Olivas Osuna, "The Deep Roots of the Carnation Revolution: 150 years of military interventionism in Portugal", *Portuguese Journal of Social Science*, 13 (2), pp.215-231.

14 Douglas L. Wheeler, "The Portuguese Army in Angola", *The Journal of Modern African Studies*, Vol.7, No.3, October 1969, pp.425-439.

15 "Military Balance", Institute of Strategic Studies (London, 1967), p.26 in Wheeler, "The Portuguese Army in Angola", pp.425-439.

16 Wheeler, *The Portuguese Army in Angola,* p.431.

17 Antonio de Spínola, *Portugal E O Future* (Peskor, 1974).

18 Fernando Andresen Guimaraes, *The Origins of the Angolan Civil War: Intervention and Domestic Political Conflict* (London: Palgrave Macmillan, 2001), p.90.

19 Spínola refused to negotiate with Neto because he claimed the MPLA was receiving instructions from Moscow. *Diário de Notícias*, 21 April 1975 in Guimaraes, *The Origins of the Angolan Civil War: Intervention and Domestic Political Conflict,* p.93.

20 Guimaraes, *The Origins of the Angolan Civil War: Intervention and Domestic Political Conflict,* p.93.

21 Mario Coelho Pinto de Andrade was the founder of the MPLA. After dispute with Agostinho Neto in 1974, he set up his own group named Active Revolt.

22 "Chronology, December 1974-February 1975", *Pakistan Horizon* (published by Pakistan Institute of International Affairs), Vol.28, No.1 (First Quarter), 1975, pp.66-143.

23 In March 1975, for example, FNLA forces gunned down fifty unarmed MPLA activists in northern Angola. John Stockwell, *In Search of Enemies* (London: Futura Publications Limited, 1979), p.68.

24 Cuban assistance to the MPLA was part of a strategy of which the intention was to expand its influence and to demonstrate its support for the recently formed Non-Aligned Movement (NAM). Nelson Valdes, "Revolutionary Solidarity in Angola", in *Cuba in the World* (eds. Cole Blasier and Carmelo Mesa-Lago) (Pittsburgh: University of Pittsburgh Press, 1979), p.91.

25 Vladimir Shubin, "The USSR and Southern Africa during the Cold War", *Centro di Studi Storica e Politica su Africa e Medio Oriente*, Occasional Paper 1, November 2008, Bologna, p.4.

26 "Soviet Military Policy in the Third World", National Intelligence Estimate, 21 October 1976, p.3.

27 Bruce D. Porter, The USSR in Third World Conflicts: Soviet Arms and Diplomacy in Local Wars, 1945– 1980 (London: Cambridge University Press, 1984), p.162.

28 Central Intelligence Agency, Directorate of Intelligence, "Soviet and Cuban Intervention in The Angolan Civil War" March 1977, p.10.

29 The Tanzanian press announced that a Soviet aircraft carrying a $6 million shipment of equipment had arrived on 1 August 1974. "Soviet and Cuban Intervention in The Angolan Civil War", p.9. Stockwell, *In Search of Enemies*, p.67, notes that the CIA speculated that these shipments were intended for Rhodesian and South African liberation movements.

30 "Soviet and Cuban Aid to the MPLA in Angola from March through December 1975", Interagency Intelligence Memorandum, 24 January 1976, p.3.

31 Chistopher Stevens, "The Soviet Union and Angola", *African Affairs*, Vol.75, No.299, April 1976, p.144.

32 Franz-Wilhelm Heimer, *The Decolonization Conflict in Angola, 1974-76: An Essay in Political Sociology* (International Studies on Contemporary Africa Series), Institut universitaire de hautes études internationales, 1979, pp.56-57.

33 Stockwell, *In Search of Enemies*, p.67.

34 Stockwell, *In Search of Enemies*, p.67.

35 Stockwell, *In Search of Enemies*, p.68.

36 Stockwell, *In Search of Enemies,* p.68.

37 Stephen L. Weigert, *Angola: A Modern Military History, 1961-2002* (London: Palgrave Macmillan, 2001), p.59.

38 Weigert, *Angola: A Modern Military History, 1961-2002,* p.59.

39 Weigert, *Angola: A Modern Military History, 1961-2002,* p.59.

40 In April 1975 when it was recognised by the OAU, the coalition of Frontline states comprised Botswana, Tanzania and Zambia.

41 Omugulugwombashe was a training base for SWAPO fighters.

42 George, *The Cuban Intervention in Angola, 1965-1991: From Che Guevara to Cuito Cuanavale*), p.62.

43 The SWALA became the PLAN in 1971.

44 Piero Gleijeses, *Conflicting Missions: Havana, Washington and Africa, 1959-1976* (Chapel Hill and London: The University of North Carolina Press, 2002), p.276.

45 George, *The Cuban Intervention in Angola, 1965-1991: From Che Guevara to Cuito Cuanavale*, p.68.

46 George, *The Cuban Intervention in Angola, 1965-1991: From Che Guevara to Cuito Cuanavale",* p.22.

47 "Speech of Dr. Fidel Castro at the UN General Assembly, September 1960", <http://www1.lanic.utexas.edu/project/castro/db/1960/19600926.html>, accessed 23 June 2018.

48 Piero Gleijeses, "Cuba's First Venture in Africa: Algeria, 1961-1965,*Journal of Latin American Studies*, 1996, p.160.

49 David Renton, David Seddon, and Leo Zelig, *The Congo: Plunder and Resistance* (London: Zed Books, 2007), p.106.

50 "Cuba Began Role in Zanzibar in '61: Havana's Part in Revolution Outlined in Washington – Guerilla Course Cited", *New York Times*, 2 January 1964.

51 George, *The Cuban Intervention in Angola, 1965-1991: From Che Guevara to Cuito Cuanavale,* p.26.

52 Dreke had fought alongside Guevara most notably in the battle to take control of Santa Clara on 31 December, 1958. Two years later, and after three days of fighting, he was captured by members of Brigade 2506 at the Bay of Pigs, only to be released at the end of the failed invasion. See, "Victor Dreke Cruz: Cuba's history man still talks of revolution", *The Independent*, 17 April, 2011.

Chapter 3

1 "President Harry S. Truman's Address before a Joint Session of Congress, March 12, 1947".

2 Peter J. Schraeder, *United States Foreign Policy Toward Africa: Incrementalism, Crisis, and Change* (New York: Cambridge University Press, 1994), p.51.

3 In July 1960, Belgian troops began military operations to protect Belgian nationals and other Europeans affected by widespread violence exacted by the Armée Nationale Congolaise (ANC).

4 "Alleged Assassination Plots Involving Foreign Leaders", An Interim Report of the Select Committee to Study Governmental Operations with Respect to Intelligence Activities (Washington: US Government Printing Office, 1975).

5 See, Stephen Rookes, *Ripe for Rebellion: Political and Military Insurgency 1946-1964* (Warwick: Helion, 2020) and Stephen Rookes, *For God and the CIA: Cuban Exile Operations in the Congo and Beyond, 1959-1967* (Warwick: Helion, 2020).

6 Bade Onimode, *A Political Economy of the African Crisis* (London: Zed Books, 1988), pp.54-55.

7 Gulf Oil, one of the Seven Sisters oil companies, was the largest single US investor in Portuguese Africa. By the end of 1972, these investments totaled some $209 million. "Letter from William Cox, Gulf Oil Corporation to Edward Hawley, 4 April 1973", in "Why We Protest Gulf Oil in Angola", *American Committee on Africa*, June 1973.

8 Ernest Harsch and Tony Thomas, *Angola: The Hidden History of Washington's War* (New York: Pathfinder Press, 1976), p.19.

9 Harsch and Thomas, *Angola: The Hidden History of Washington's War*, p.19.

10 "*Military Facilities in the Azores: Agreement between Portugal and the United States*", 6 September 1951, American Foreign Policy 1950-1955, Basic Documents Volumes I and II, Department of State Publication 6446, General Foreign Policy Series 117, Washington, DC : U.S. Government Printing Office, 1957.

11 "Azores Agreement Means Increased US Backing of Colonial Wars", *American Committee on Africa*, 10 December 1971.

12 The CIA believed that Portugal might have been able to hold its position for several years to come but that eventually the political and military costs would force it "to accommodate nationalist aspirations for self-determination and independence". "Short-Term Prospects for the Africain Nationalist Movements in Angola and Mozambique", Special National Intelligence Estimate, Number 71-64, 1 July 1964, pp.1-13.

13 "Country Summary Prepared in the Bureau of Intelligence Research, Washington, 6 March 1967", Document 442, FRUS, 1964-1968, Vol. XXIV, Africa.

14 "Short-Term Prospects for the Africain Nationalist Movements in Angola and Mozambique".

15 "Alleged Assassination Plots involving Foreign Leaders", p.18

16 "National Security Council Meeting" Washington, 25 July 1960, Central Intelligence Agency Files, Job 79R00890A, Box 13, Folder 1, NSC Briefings, July 1960. Top Secret; [codeword not declassified].

17 Tim Weiner, *Legacy of the Ashes: The History of the CIA* (New York: Anchor, 2008), p.162.

18 The naval force in question comprised Cuban exiles.

19 Roberto married a woman from the same village as Mobutu's wife.

20 John Marcum, *The Angolan Revolution, Volume II: Exile Politics and Guerilla Warfare*, 1962-1976 (Michigan, USA: The MIT Press, 1978), p.259.
21 Georges Nzongola-Ntalaja, *The Congo from Leopold to Kabila: A People's History* (London: Zed Books, 2002), p.148.
22 Vance, Kinshasa to Secretary of State, "Dini on Prospects of Congolese Economy", 2 July 1970, RG 59, Economic, Box 787, Department of State, NARA II, in Bechtolsheimer, Breakfast with Mobutu: Congo, the United States and the Cold war, 1964-1981, p.90.
23 "Memorandum of Conversation", Meeting with Congo (K) President Mobutu: Portugal and Angola (Part 3 of 5), Washington, 4 August 1970, NARA, RG 59, Central files, 1970-73, POL 17, The Congo, Secret.
24 "USSR-Africa: Soviets Increasing Aid to African Liberation Fronts"?, Washington, 11 August 1970. Department of State, INR/IL Historical files, Africa, Latin America, Inter-Agency Intelligence Committee Files, Angola-Washington, Secret.
25 "US-Zaire Relations", Washington, 12 August 1974. Library of Congress, Manuscript Division, Kissinger Papers, Box CL 257, Geopolitical File, Zaire, August 1974-June 1975.
26 "US-Zaire Relations", 12 August 1974.
27 "US-Zaire Relations", 12 August 1974.
28 "US-Zaire Relations", 12 August 1974.
29 "Mobutu's Request for Material Support to Holden Roberto", Washington, 19 September 1974. Ford Library, National Security Adviser, Outside the System Chronological File, Box 1.
30 "Mobutu's Request for Material Support to Holden Roberto", 19 September 1974.
31 Stockwell, *In Search of Enemies*, p.274. Also see, "40 Committee Decisions", Department of State, INR/IL Historical Files, Intelligence Committee Report File, 40 Committee, 22 January 1975.
32 John Marcum, "Lessons of Angola", *Foreign Affairs*, 54, April 1976, pp.407-425.
33 "United States Policy Toward Angola", Washington, 26 May 1975. Ford Library, National Security Adviser, NSDMs and NSSMs, Box 2, NSSMs File, NSSM 224.
34 "United States Policy Toward Angola", 26 May 1975.
35 Christopher John Lamb, *Belief Systems and Decision Making in the Mayaguez Crisis* (Gainesville: University of Florida Press, 1989), p.241 in Thomas J. Noer, "International Credibility and Political Survival: The Ford Administration's Intervention in Angola", *Presidential Studies Quarterly*, Fall, 1993, Vol.23, No.4, pp.771-785.
36 Seymour M. Hersh, "Huge CIA Operation Reported in US Against Antiwar Forces, other Dissidents in Nixon Years", *New York Times*, 22 December 1974.
37 The committee became known as such due to its being headed by Senator Frank Church (D-ID).
38 "40 Committee Meeting", 5 June 1975. National Security Council, Ford Administration Intelligence Files, 40 Committee Meetings, Secret.
39 "40 Committee Meeting", 5 June 1975.
40 "Private Meeting between UNITA President Savimbi and Zairian President Mobutu", 9 June 1975. Library of Congress Manuscript Division, Kissinger Papers, Box CL 102, Geopolitical File, Angola Chronological File.
41 "Angola", Washington, 11 June 1975. Library of Congress Manuscript Division, Kissinger Papers, Box CL 102, Geopolitical File, Angola Chronological File.
42 "Angola", Washington, 11 June 1975.
43 "Angola", Washington, 11 June 1975.
44 "Angola", Washington, 11 June 1975.
45 "Angola", Washington, 11 June 1975.
46 "Response to NSSM 224: United States Policy Toward Angola", Washington, 13 June 1975, Department of State, INR/IL Historical Files, Africa, Latin America, Inter-Agency Intelligence Committee Files, Angola, NSSM 224, Papers, Secret.
47 "Africa", Washington, 20 June 1975. Library of Congress Manuscript Division, Kissinger Papers, Box CL 102, Geopolitical File, Angola Chronological File.
48 "Africa", 20 June 1975.
49 "Africa", 20 June 1975.
50 "Africa", 20 June 1975.
51 "Minutes of a National Security Council Meeting", Washington, 27 June 1975. Ford Library, National Security Advisor, NSC Meetings File, Box 2, NSC Meeting, 27 June 1975.
52 "Minutes of a National Security Council Meeting", 27 June 1975.
53 "Minutes of a National Security Council Meeting", 27 June 1975.
54 "40 Committee Meeting, 14 July 1975, National Security Council, Ford Administration Intelligence Files, 40 Committee Meetings, Secret.
55 "Plan for Covert Action -Angola", Department of State, INR/IL Historical Files, Africa, Latin America, Inter-Agency Intelligence Committee Files, Angola-Washington, Secret; Sensitive.
56 "Memorandum of Conversation", Washington, 17 July 1975. Library of Congress, Manuscript Division, Kissinger Papers, Box CL 282, Memoranda of Conversations, Presidential File, 17 July 1975.
57 "Telegram from the Embassy in Zaire to the Department of State", Kinshasa, 24 July 1975. National Archives, RG 59, Central Foreign Policy Files, P840178 – 1917.
58 "Memorandum of Conversation", Washington, 25 July 1975. Library of Congress, Manuscript Division, Kissinger Papers, Box CL 102, Geopolitical File, Angola Chronological File.
59 "Memorandum from the Executive Secretary of the 40 Committee (Ratliff) to Director of Central Intelligence Colby", 28 July 1975. Natioanl Security Council, Ford Administration Intelligence Files, 40 Committee meetings.
60 Stockwell, *In Search of Enemies*, p.53.
61 Stockwell, *In Search of Enemies*, pp.25-27.
62 Victor Flintham, *Air Wars and Aircraft: A Detailed Record of Air Combat, 1945 to the Present* (London: Arms and Armour Press, 1989), p.216.
63 Stockwell, *In Search of Enemies*, p.57.
64 "40 Committee Meeting", 8 August 1975. National Security Council, Ford Administration, Intelligence Files, 40 Committee Meetings; Secret; Eyes Only.
65 Stockwell, *In Search of Enemies*, p.166.
66 Flintham, *Air Wars and Aircraft*, p.117.
67 Stockwell, *In Search of Enemies*, p.169.
68 Stockwell, *In Search of Enemies*, p.170.
69 George, *The Cuban Intervention in Angola*, p.104.

Chapter 4

1 "Branaman Chronology".
2 Gelb, *New York Times*, 3 October 1976.
3 "Branaman Chronology", in "Mercenaries in Africa", Hearing before the Subcommittee on Investigations of the Committee

on International Relations, House of Representatives, 94th Congress, Washington, 9 August 1976.

4 "Walker Chronology" in Mark M. Lowenthal, "Foreign Assistance in the Angolan Civil War: Chronology of Reported Events, 1975-1976", Congressional Research Service (CRS) Library of Congress, 8 June 1976, entry for 17 November 1975.

5 "CRS Chronology", entry for 17 November 1975.

6 "CRS Chronology", entry for 17 November 1975.

7 "40 Committee Meeting, 14 November 1975", National Security Council, Ford Administration, Intelligence Files, 40 Committee Meetings.

8 Flintham, *Air Wars and Aircraft,* p.117 & Fontanellaz et all, *War of Intervention in Angola, Vol.3*, pp.12-15

9 "Memorandum of Conversation", 19 November 1975, Kissinger Papers, Box CL 103, Geopolitical File, Angola Chronological File.

10 "CRS Chronology", entry for 26 November 1975 & Fontanellaz et all, *War of Intervention in Angola, Vol.3*, pp.12-15

11 David Binder, *New York Times*, 13 December 1975, as quoted in "CRS Chronology", entry for 4 December 1975.

12 "Branaman Chronology", entry for 27 November 1975.

13 "40 Committee Meeting", 21 November 1975, NSC, Ford Administration Files, Intelligence Files, 40 Committee Meetings.

14 "Branaman Chronology" entry for 7 December 1975.

15 "Branaman Chronology" entry for 12 December 1975.

16 "Branaman Chronology" entry for 14 December 1975.

17 Thomas A. Johnson, *New York Times*, 11 February 1976.

18 "Branaman Chronology" entry for 10 December 1975.

19 "CRS Chronology", entry for 12 December 1975.

20 "CRS Chronology", entry for 12 December 1975.

21 Robin Wright, "Talkative Mercenary Claims CIA Tie", *The Washington Post*, 6 May 1977.

22 Rose Marie Royal, "Mercenaries' Time in Angola Disputed", *The Lantern*, 15 July 1976.

23 "40 Committee Meeting, 14 November 1975".

24 "Hearings before the Subcommittee on Africa of the Committee on Foreign Affairs, House of Representatives", 96th Congress, 17-30 September 1980.

25 Jane Franklin, *Cuba and the US Empire: A Chronological History* (New York: Monthly Review Press, 2016), entry for 31 December 1975.

26 Laurence Stern, "The Angola Mercenary Caper", *Washington Post*, 9 January 1976.

27 A. Calvão, "De Conacry ao MDLP", dossier secreto, *Intervenção*, Lisbon, 1976, in Gisele Lobato, "The Strange Case of Brazilian Support to the FNLA in the Final Stage of Angolan Decolonization", *afriche e oriente*, Number 3, 2017, p.34.

28 Stockwell, *In Search of Enemies*, pp.133-134.

29 Stockwell, *In Search of Enemies*, p.188.

30 "Memorandum of conversation", Washington, 19 November 1975, Library of Congress, Manuscript Division, Kissinger Papers, Box CL 103.

31 Stockwell, *In Search of Enemies*, p.189.

32 Stephen Dorril, *MI6: Inside the Covert World of Her Majesty's Secret Intelligence Service* (London: Free Press, 2002), p.265.

33 Stockwell, *In Search of Enemies,* p.190.

34 Stockwell, *In Search of Enemies*, p.234.

35 "Memorandum of Conversation", Washington, 18 December 1975, "Kissinger Papers, Box CL 103".

36 Stockwell, *In Search of Enemies*, pp.234-235.

37 Chris Dempster & Dave Tomkins with Michel Parry, *Fire Power* (London: Corgi Books, 1978), p.22

38 A former member of *Les Affreux* who fought for Moïse Tshombé in Katanga in 1960-1963, Masy had invested his earnings in a bar and now served beer to an array of former colonial fighters from around the world.

39 After Indochina and Algeria, "Leon" had allegedly served in the Congo under Bob Denard in 6 Commando.

40 This section was adapted from Chris Dempster and Dave Tomkins, *Fire Power* (London: Corgi Books, 1978), and John Banks, *The Wages of War: The Life of a Modern Mercenary* (London: Leo Cooper, 1978).

41 Sometimes referred to as Mervyn Hall and Norman Mervyn Hall.

42 Dempster and Tomkins, *Fire Power*, pp.55-56.

43 Dempster and Tomkins, *Fire Power*, p.61.

44 The *Irish Times* of 15 December 2000 states that Georgiou was identified by civilian and military witnesses at the Saville Inquiry into events that took place on 30 January 1972. An article that appeared in *The Irish News* also states that Hall and Banks may have taken part in the Ballymurphy massacre in August 1971 in which ten Catholic civilians were killed by the Parachute Regiment. See, Connia Young, "Para torture victim demands British apology", *The Irish News*, 22 July 2015.

45 Costas Georgiou was born on 21 December 1951.

46 This is the address given by Georgiou during the Luanda Trial held in June 1976.

47 Dempster and Tomkins, *Fire Power*, p.64.

48 Dempster and Tomkins, *Fire Power*, p.64.

49 Two of the publications produced by the Mozambique and Guinea Information Centre were "People's Power in Mozambique and Guinea-Bissau", and "Mozambique Revolution".

50 Dempster and Tomkins, *Fire Power*, p.65.

51 Referred to as "George Cullen" by Stockwell, *In Search of Enemies*, pp.237, *Callan* was the name of a popular British television series starring Edward Woodward that was aired between 1967 and 1972.

52 Dempster and Tomkins, *Fire Power*, p.69. Callan also worked at a hospital in Ambriz.

53 According to Dempster and Tomkins, this was not the first aircraft Portuguese mercenaries had stolen. Earlier, they hijacked three F.27s and a Beech Baron at Luanda Airport. Dempster and Tomkins, *Fire Power*, p.72.

54 It is not made clear if these mercenaries were some of those recruited by David Bufkin. Dempster and Tomkins, *Fire Power*, p.74, state that these Americans were withdrawn from Angola after protests made by officials in Washington.

55 "CRS Chronology", entry for 17 December 1975.

56 One of only two references in literature to Fernandes appears in *Africa Diary, 1983* (Michigan, USA: University of Michigan, 1983), p.11271. According to this reference, Fernandes was serving with UNITA as late as 1977. The confusion may be related to Victor Fernandes having a brother serving with the FNLA. See, Dempster and Tomkins, *Fire Power*, p.76.

57 Dempster and Tomkins, *Fire Power*, p.77.

58 *Christian Science Monitor* as referenced in "CRS Chronology", entry for 1 January 1976.

59 In Dempster and Tomkins, *Fire Power*, p.80, "Jean-Pierre" is described as a fifty-year-old Frenchman born in Marseilles and educated at a British public school.

60 The Binza district of Kinshasa provided the name for a group of Congolese politicians and officials with close links to the CIA during the Congo Crisis, 1960-1967. The Binza Group included Mobutu, and former Congolese prime ministers Joseph Iléo and Cyrille Adoula.
61 Leslie Aspin, with Trevor Aspinall, *I, Kovaks* (London: Everest Books Limited, 1975).
62 Aspin, *I, Kovaks*, p.10.
63 Peter McAleese, *No Mean Soldier* (London, Orion Books Ltd, 1993).
64 This was a plan that involved Libya's Colonel Gaddafi shipping weapons to the IRA. The name of the boat carrying these weapons was the *Claudia*.
65 Not to be confused with the American politician of the same name.
66 John Loftus and Mark Aarons, *The Secret War Against the Jews: How Western Espionage Betrayed the Jewish People* (New York: St Martin's Griffin,1994).
67 John Loftus and Mark Aarons, *The Secret War Against the Jews: How Western Espionage Betrayed the Jewish People,* p.380.
68 John Loftus and Mark Aarons, *The Secret War Against the Jews: How Western Espionage Betrayed the Jewish People,* pp.386-387.
69 "The Robert Vesco Investigation", aka, "Hearings before the Permanent Subcommittee on Investigations of the Committee on Government Operations, United States Senate", 22 July, 17 September, and 7 October 1974, p.29.
70 Dempster and Tomkins, *Fire Power*, p.93.
71 "CIA Supplied Mercenaries Fight in Angola", *Washington Office on Africa* (undated) early February 1976 < https://projects.kora.matrix.msu.edu/files/210-808-367/woaciaang.pdf>, accessed 5 April 2021.
72 Dempster and Tomkins, *Fire Power*, p.89.
73 Dempster and Tomkins, *Fire Power*, p.90.
74 Dempster and Tomkins, *Fire Power*, p.92.
75 Dempster and Tomkins, *Fire Power*, p.93.
76 Two others were associates of Banks, Aspin and Perren. The first, Terence Haig, was an ex-Royal Marine who presented himself as the spokesman fro the FNLA in England; and the second was James Hilton. The evidence presented at the Luanda Trial makes it clear that both had knowledge that SAS was being funded by American money transferred through Roberto and Mobutu. See court proceedings in Mike J. Hoover, "The Laws of War and the Angolan Trial of Mercenaries: Death to the Dogs of War", *Case Western Reserve Journal of International Law*, Volume 9, Issue 2, 1977, p.375.
77 Dempster and Tomkins, *Fire Power*, p.95.
78 McAleese, *No Mean Soldier*, p.64.
79 Dempster and Tomkins, *Fire Power*, p.100.
80 For more on the British government's possible complicity in assisting mercenaries to leave the UK without passports see Wilfred Burchett & Derek Roebuck, *The Whores of War: Mercenaries Today* (London: Penguin Books, 1977), pp.41-51.
81 According to the Canadian government, Newby was not a mercenary but a journalist on assignment in Angola for the French magazine *Paris Match*. See, < https://www.lipad.ca/full/1977/05/04/4/>, accessed 27 March 2021.
82 "Episode 17: Good Guys, Bad Guys, Interview with Dave Tomkins", < https://nsarchive2.gwu.edu/coldwar/interviews/episode-17/tomkins1.html>, accessed 27 March 2021.
83 Stockwell, *In Search of Enemies*, pp.235-236. Here, Stockwell also confirms that mercenary leaders met with CIA officers in Kinshasa and used safe houses used during IA/FEATURE.
84 McAleese, *No Mean Soldier*, p.75.
85 Dempster and Tomkins, *Fire Power*, pp.164-165.
86 Dempster and Tomkins, *Fire Power*, p.168
87 Dempster and Tomkins, *Fire Power*, pp.164-165.
88 McAleese, *No Mean Soldier*, p.71.
89 McAleese, *No Mean Soldier*, p.71.
90 *The Washington Post*, 6 February 1976 in CRS Chronology, entry for 22 January 1976.
91 The *New York Times*, 26 January 1976, in CRS Chronology, entry for 25 January 1976 (sic).
92 Dempster and Tomkins, *Fire Power*, pp.176-177.
93 José R. Alfonso, "People's Republic of Angola: Combat de Damba. Quibocolo-Angola Ambush, 1976, Part III", < http://www.codigoabierto360.com/republica-popular-de-angola-combate-de-damba-emboscada-de-quibocolo-angola-1976/>, accessed 30 March 2021.
94 Dempster and Tomkins, *Fire Power*, p.205.
95 Dempster and Tomkins, *Fire Power*, p.319.
96 In another account, the name of the victim is given as David Wileman. Bruchett and Roebuck, *Whores of War*, p.105.
97 Dempster and Tomkins, *Fire Power*, p.343.
98 Vic Gawthorp died of a heart-attack while in the Land Rover while Max Risbridger is thought to have been one of the other killed. The identity of the third deceased is not known, but sources give the names of the seriously wounded as 'Geordie' Jones and Denis O'Brien. The mine had been laid by the FNLA.
99 Burchett and Roebuck, *Whores of War*, p.107.
100 There are three villages lying between Quibocolo and Damba: Bango, Banza, and Banza Lala.
101 The dates of the attacks on Cuban/FAPLA forces vary according to the source.
102 Dempster and Tomkins, *Fire Power*, p.343.
103 Dempster and Tomkins, *Fire Power*, p.363 give the date as 2 February. This seems chronologically impossible and contradicts accounts given by Kevin Marchant in Burchett and Roebuck, *Whores of War*, p.109, who gives the date as 5 February 1976.
104 Dempster and Tomkins, *Fire Power*, p.364. See the earlier account of a battle occurring in late January provided in Cuban sources. It would appear in these sources that the dates of the two battles have been confused as it refers to 24 mercenaries being killed. Alfonso, "People's Republic of Angola: Combat de Damba. Quibocolo-Angola Ambush, 1976, Part III". On the other hand, this source gives the date of Callan's last attack on Cuban forces as 5 February. This date is supported by Kevin Marchant's testimonial as noted in Burchett and Roebuck, *Whores of War*, p.109.
105 Dempster and Tomkins, *Fire Power*, p.365.
106 Dempster and Tomkins, *Fire Power*, p.366.
107 Burchett and Roebuck, *Whores of War*, p.108.
108 It is possible that this was a soldier known only as S. Arnold.
109 CIA-Supplied Mercenaries Fight in Angola", *Washington Office on Africa* (undated) early February 1976, < https://projects.kora.matrix.msu.edu/files/210-808-367/woaciaang.pdf>, accessed 5 April 1976.
110 Stockwell, *In Search of Enemies*, p.247. Also see the discussions led by Kissinger and held in Washington on the day the Tunney Amendment. Here, it was proposed that money from a Saudi

oil deal could be used to buy equipment and fund mercenary recruitment. "Memorandum of Conversation", 19 December 1975, Kissinger Papers, Box CL 103.
111 Stockwell, *In Search of Enemies*, p.247.
112 "CRS Chronology", entry for 5 February 1976.
113 "CRS Chronology", entry for 6 February 1976.
114 "CRS Chronology", entry for 16 February 1976.
115 Robin Wright, "Talkative Mercenary Claims CIA Tie", *Washington Post*, 6 May 1977.
116 The Military Assistance Command, Vietnam – Studies and Observations Group was a highly classified special operations group active in South Vietnam, North Vietnam, Cambodia and Laos.
117 For more on the life and activities of George Bacon III see, Jack Murphy, "MACV – SOG Operator, CIA Para-Military Officer, Mercenary, and Genius", *Sofrep*, 24 May 2012, < https://sofrep.com/news/george-washington-bacon-part-1/>, accessed 6 April 2021.
118 Moss, Bacon, Malloy, Farman*, Dickens, Young, Sharpley, Atkins, Kavac, Patay, Henderson, and a medic named Simanin. No reference can be found to a "Farman" in the works used for this study. This list taken from Newby's diary (Burchett and Roebuck, *Whores of War*, p.114), Dempster and Tomkins give Acker as being part of this group. See, Dempster and Tomkins, *Fire Power*, pp.428-429.
119 "Telegram from Secretary of State Kissinger to the Embassy in France", 14 February 1976, National Archives, RG 59, Central Foreign Policy Files, P840086-1506.
120 "CRS Chronology", entry for 19 February 1976.
121 "Report Prepared by the Working Group on Angola", *Military Matériel Sent to Zaire Under the Angola Covert Paramilitary Program*, Washington, 20 February 1976, Kissinger Papers, Box CL 104.
122 CRS Chronology", entry for 20 February.
123 Stockwell, *In Search of Enemies*, p.255.
124 "CRS Chronology", entry for 14 March 1976.
125 "Report Prepared by the Working Group on Angola", Washington, 2 April 1976, Kissinger Papers, Box CL 104.
126 Stockwell, *In Search of Enemies*, pp.260-261.
127 George H. Lockwood, "Report on the Trial of Mercenaries", Luanda, Angola – June, 1976
128 Dempster and Tomkins, *Fire Power*, p.460.
129 Lockwood, "Report on the Trial of Mercenaries".

About the Author

Dr. Stephen Rookes is an Anglo-French researcher working at the French Air Force officer training academy in Salon-de-Provence, France. He has produced a number of academic articles in English and in French and specialises in the history of warfare in Africa as well as CIA clandestine operations since 1947. This is his third book for Helion.